Lots of love

X

DADS

DADS

A Celebration of Fatherhood from
Britain's Finest and Funniest

Edited by Sarah Brown and Gil McNeil

EBURY
PRESS

3 5 7 9 10 8 6 4 2

Published in 2008 by Ebury Press, an imprint of Ebury Publishing
A Random House Group Company

Collection copyright © PiggyBankKids Projects 2008

Each contributor has asserted their right to be identified
as the author of their contribution in accordance with
the Copyright, Designs and Patents Act 1988

Illustrations by Simon Stern

The Random House Group Limited Reg. No. 954009

Addresses for companies within the Random House Group
can be found at www.randomhouse.co.uk

A CIP catalogue record for this book is available from the British Library

The Random House Group Limited supports The Forest Stewardship
Council (FSC), the leading international forest certification organisation.
All our titles that are printed on Greenpeace approved FSC certified paper
carry the FSC logo. Our paper procurement policy can be found at
www.rbooks.co.uk/environment

Designed and set by seagulls.net

Printed in the UK by CPI Mackays, Chatham, ME5 8TD

ISBN 9780091922726

To buy books by your favourite authors and register for offers visit
www.rbooks.co.uk

CONTENTS

FOREWORD
Sarah Brown

I am greatly indebted to all the contributors to this book, which is a wonderful and unique collection of thoughts and musings about dads.

Everyone here has given their piece for this book in support of PiggyBankKids, who will receive all the royalties from book sales. The charity supports a range of projects creating opportunities for children and young people, from mentoring programmes to sports activities to cancer care help. A major part of the charity's work is through the Jennifer Brown Research Fund, which supports pioneering medical research to save and improve newborn lives where there are pregnancy and birth difficulties.

Buying this collection to support this work is a good act in itself, but truthfully the book is well worth the read anyway. It has been a real privilege for me to ask some of my favourite people to contribute to this anthology; even better when they said yes, and the result turns out to be a stunning collection of frank recollections and a combination of touching and funny tales. My heartfelt thanks to all.

I would also like to thank my husband Gordon for his introduction to this book. Do I think asking the Prime Minister to write the introduction will sell more copies? Given its contribution to the work of PiggyBankKids, I certainly hope so. Of course, I understand that I am prevailing on the time of a very busy person in whom everyone has a stake, but I remember his father so well, and wanted to include Gordon's thoughts on him in the book. Gordon is also everything I could have wished for as the father of our two boys – patient, fun, encouraging and always interested in their small lives – and much of that comes from his upbringing.

One of my saddest times ever was making the call to tell him that his dad was gone. He was such an important figure in the life of Gordon and his brothers that with his loss a moment arrived when everything changed. In losing my father in 2007 I understood better the sudden exposure you feel when one of the central pillars of your life suddenly is no longer there to hold the sky above you.

I have been fortunate to have had a close relationship with my dad and my stepfather since I was a young child. A case of doubling up on a good thing I think. My brother, Sean Macaulay, is a writer so I have left it to him to better capture the benefits of both. I am a great fan of my brother at the best of times, but he is particularly good at being a dad himself. He is the kind that thinks nothing of roaring around on his hands and knees for hours on end just because his little girls and their cousins think it is hilarious; the best kind.

I would also like to thank my co-editor Gil McNeil for helping guide and co-ordinate the task of creating this book; Joe Hewitt for his great contribution to PiggyBankKids in managing our programme of work; and the Trustees of the charity, Lord Paul, David Boutcher, Baroness Goudie, Jim O'Neill, Helen Scott Lidgett and Arabella Weir, who do so much to further the work of PiggyBankKids. Thank you too to the numerous people involved in all aspects of the charity's work, notably Professor Andrew Calder, Dr Ian Laing, Dr Rhona Hughes and the team at the Jennifer Brown Research Laboratory, and Dr Tahir Mahmood and the team behind the community programme of the Jennifer Brown Fife Appeal.

And finally a thank you to the team at Ebury Press including Gail Rebuck who always keeps the faith with my various projects, Fiona McIntyre, Hannah MacDonald, Rae Shirvington and Sarah Bennie, and everyone else at Ebury, who put so much energy into all our publishing projects.

INTRODUCTION
Gordon Brown, Prime Minister

Some years after my father died, I received a letter from Bill Martin telling me how much my father had helped him decades ago, when Bill was a teenager in Govan and my father was his parish minister.

I knew a fair amount about Bill – the hugely successful songwriter who wrote 'Congratulations', 'Puppet on a String', a whole clutch of Eurovision Song Contest winners, and numerous other hits in the 1960s and 1970s – but was intrigued to learn from his letter what he had to say about my father.

How could my father, a Presbyterian clergyman, famously tone-deaf and with no knowledge of popular music, ever have helped Bill Martin on his way to becoming a pop legend and one of the most famous songwriters of his generation?

Bill grew up in a Govan tenement, and from the age

of ten had ambitions to become a songwriter, but left school at 15 to work in a shipyard. He explained how as a teenager he was easily discouraged and unsure of his way in the world, and wanted to tell me all those years later that it was my father who had encouraged him to believe in his talent, to use it, and make the most of wherever it took him.

And when I read Bill's letter, I thought: that makes two of us. My father was responsible for so much of what I am – and what I believe. Everyone, he used to say, has a talent; everyone should have the chance to see that talent flourish and to make their mark one way or another.

People may think of a Church of Scotland upbringing as probably grim and dour – and certainly Calvinist. That wasn't my father at all. His personal faith was optimistic and outgoing, and his interest in people, his sympathy for their concerns, and his faith in their potential reflected that.

In each of the parishes he served, our home was visited endlessly by people in search of his advice or support, often at the best or worst times of their lives. His pastoral care was instinctive and genuine. And he and my mother made a wonderful team, her commitment to helping other people the cornerstone of her life, and young people setting out in the world heard wisdom and encouragement. The bereaved found solace and comfort. And teenagers like Bill were helped to believe in themselves and what they could achieve.

My father was also – by the standards of his calling – remarkably good-humoured, with a real talent for cheering people up, and a loud and ready laugh to go with it. And – though he never touched alcohol, because he had seen too much of the damage it could do – he could be the life and soul of any party.

A few weeks after his death, my brother found some typed pages: my father's attempt at the first chapter of an autobiography.

He must have started it when he was already in his eighties, and to our disappointment he didn't get very far beyond his school and university days. But what this manuscript revealed was the journey of an only son who had lost his mother when he was a teenager – and whose father then had to make real sacrifices so that he could be the first in his family to go to university.

It was the 1930s and my grandfather was at the time

unemployed. He had some savings, just enough to get by. In the coming years, when he was back on his feet, he helped my father again and again: to set up a home and buy his first car; and then to bring up a family on a parish minister's salary. And I remember the quiet love between them, as strong as ever on the last day of my grandfather's life, when my father took me, then just eight years old, to see him and to say goodbye.

In our family, as in so many others, there is a tacitly accepted but unbreakable chain of values that links us across the generations. I felt that again – perhaps never more strongly – as I read that fragment of autobiography. Incomplete as it was, my father's character was there in it, complete and unmistakable. What came through most of all were his gratitude and his sense of obligation.

In these old-fashioned typed pages, he fondly remembered what his teachers had done for him; and proudly recounted how his parents had put his interests before their own – especially in how his father made sure he could make the most of his talents by going to university. That mattered enormously to him: it shaped his life and enabled him to live it in the service of others. And I remember how he felt when his old university summoned him to receive an honorary doctorate. He said it was the only honour he truly valued.

But I know that there was something else he prized: I saw the delight in his face when I told him that a selection of his sermons had been published in a small book. In them, there was the other side of who he was: not what he had been given, but his commitment to give something back. His whole ministry – 45 years in just four parishes – was directed not at preaching down to people, but to lifting them up.

There was one stormy day when the waves crashed over Kirkcaldy's harbour walls. He took me along as he visited families who had been flooded out and evacuated from their homes. He comforted them: he brought hope – and blankets, and food, and a bit of money – at a time of despair. And throughout his ministry everyone in need who ever came to our door was treated with dignity and no one left empty-handed.

My father had an innate and sometimes surprising sense of fairness. When I was just seven, he took me to see my first match at my beloved Raith Rovers against out local rivals East Fife; but I was confused to see him applauding both sides, and asked, 'Why are you clapping for them?' His answer – that you should applaud good play from whatever side – showed a generosity of spirit that most of us can only admire.

He was generous to us, his sons, in countless small ways. Every Saturday night when my brothers and I were growing up, he walked down to the high street and brought back the evening sporting papers for his football-mad sons – all three of us – so that we could study the football results. And later on, when my mother was seriously ill – over two difficult years in the 1960s – he did the work of two parents for his three teenage sons, everything from cooking our breakfast in the morning to checking on our homework before we went to bed.

My father never lectured us, never demanded we do things or threatened. He didn't try to impose his views on us, but you did know when he was disappointed.

The same concern he showed us, people tell me, radiated out to so many others in our community. In his life as a parish minister he lived out a consistent and heartening message in many different ways: look to the best in yourself, and look to something bigger than yourself, and find fulfilment in service to others.

His sermons always seemed to reflect that, and were carefully prepared – but only at the last minute. Every Sunday morning, his routine was the same. The church bell would have begun ringing before he left his study, where he typed with two fingers and what he called 'the inspiration of desperation'; but he was never late for the service, which every week began promptly at 11 o'clock. I believe I have inherited his two-finger typing style, and his sometimes risk-taking approach to deadlines, but not – sadly, or at least not yet – his punctuality.

Ten years ago my father set out on a very cold winter morning to post a small Christmas gift to an old lady he had kept in touch with since first meeting her during his ministry in Dunoon in the 1950s. On the way home he collapsed and died. The night before, he had phoned me, and we said we would talk the next day. We never did; but in my heart, I still hear his voice, his kindliness, his wisdom and the recurrent theme of his sermons and – more importantly – his life.

It's only when your parents are gone that you realise how much you had assumed they would always be there for you, as permanent as rock.

And then you find the seemingly immortal is mortal after all and that nothing physical endures.

And the shock of the passing is the void that opens up when they've gone. And only when my father died did I realise how much he had influenced me – how I tested ideas by thinking of what he might think of them: how they would measure up to his ideals and his values. And ten years on, I do it still.

The BBC correspondent Angus Roxburgh wrote movingly of his father's death, pointing out that when parents die you find there is 'Nothing between us and the stars... Suddenly you become the last line of defence. Even if as an adult you scarcely looked any more to your parents for support or advice, there is suddenly a void when they are gone. There's no one ahead of you; your generation becomes the oldest... When our parents die a link to the eternal is lost, a link to the past, to the great mysteries that die with them. Now you're on your own. Just you. And the stars.'

But you are not entirely left on your own. You hold on to what you have been given. As my brother said at my father's funeral, our father not only gave us a moral compass; he was our moral compass. He still is, and always will be – and what he has given me – the values, the faith in the future – I hope as the father of two young children to pass on to them, and then them to the next generation too. Nothing can ever rival or match the joy of becoming a father, and knowing what I can pass on to my children only adds to that.

Roger Alton

Fathers and sons. Fathers and sons. It's all about cricket. Fathers have a sacred duty to teach their sons about cricket: to love it, to watch it, to talk about it (interminably), and, with luck, play it. It's the law. You can see it all over the land through Britain's half-arsed summers: from Taunton to Trent Bridge, from Cardiff to Chester–le–Street. Small groups of men in the deserted stands, muffled in anoraks against the cold, cheerful youngsters looking on eagerly: sharing squash and sandwiches, between the showers, between the innings, before the rush for the last bus home. It's the way it's meant to be.

The other night, unpleasant and sleepless in the freezing January small hours, I settled down in front of the telly to watch brilliant, live, vivid Test cricket from a sunbathed Sydney. Australia vs. India. I thought of Dad and wished he'd been there.

He used to take me to the Parks in Oxford in the

endless summer of a fifties' childhood. Free of course. We'd plonk down in deck-chairs, Dad and I, and watch the University play the touring teams, Australia, India, South Africa. Unbelievable. And such a privilege.

He was no mean cricketer, Dad. He played Minor Counties cricket, and captained innumerable club sides. He was a well-loved leader of men. A decorated war hero, and a fine academic, and he did love his cricket. We'd drive off every Sunday morning. Eight-year-old me, Dad, and some of the other players: they would have been students, just kids, but to me they were like gods. If I said something that made them laugh, I was in heaven. I am not sure how pleased Mum was about all this. Not very, I discovered as the years rolled by.

Later I used to take him to watch Test matches, at Lord's and the Oval. But he wasn't moving too well then. I think he enjoyed it, though. It's a damn shame when the light starts to dim. A crying shame.

He had a funny action, Dad: he was a very good off-spinner but he approached the wicket at anything between 45 and maybe 60 degrees. Almost out of the batsman's line of vision. It was weird. This was why: because when he was a kid, learning to play cricket in the family backyard in a little town in the East Midlands, there was only room for an 18-yard pitch. To get a run-up, Dad had to go side-on. And he worked and worked at it; he wouldn't give up. He was good though: I'm looking at a scorecard now. Dad captained the Incogniti vs. Douai school in June 1966. He took 6 for 29, and the cricket master complained. He was a cunning old bugger, Dad. But as fair as the day is long. I miss him very much. Who can I burble about cricket with now?

Fathers and daughters though...that's a different matter.

'What do you think of cricket?' I asked Hannah, my beautiful and cool teenaged daughter.

'Well, I've got a cricket sweater.'

'And...'

'It's fabulous.'

So you see, the tradition lives on. Sort of.

Cheers, Dad. Here's to you.

Roger Alton is a journalist and former Editor of the Observer.

Christiane Amanpour

I was recently honoured to receive a CBE from Queen Elizabeth II, and after the Buckingham Palace investiture, I thanked my parents for the fantastic childhood they had given me that sustains me through thick and thin to this day. My father, who is now 93 years old, features prominently in my earliest memories. He is from Iran and I was raised there in a world of adventure, fun and love, combined with fairness, truth and morality. One of my earliest influences was horse-riding. My father found one of his old army buddies from his cavalry days to take me riding, and the process instilled a lifelong sense of discipline, courage, compassion and respect for the power of another living thing. I also learned the thrill of accomplishment and the ability to rise each time I fell…or was thrown off.

My father was very funny and a good linguist who was always telling me stories and singing songs in English, French, German, and sometimes even Russian! Growing up in Iran there was not much television, but I always remember my father glued to the set for the imported nature programmes. His sense of awe at the antics and habitats of the lions, cheetahs, snakes and bears was infectious, and to this day I practically drop everything to watch that type of programme. I am trying to instil the same habit in my son. To learn to love the beauty and magnificence of our planet, and its fantastic plants and creatures, is critical now more than ever, as we humans struggle to reach a sense of accommodation with our environment, and hopefully save it.

I think the most important thing my father gave me was unconditional love and approval. He never urged me along a particular career path, never acted as though I ever fell short of parental expectations, never made me feel I had to prove anything. This was liberating and allowed me to find my own level in the world, to pursue my ambitions and to thrive. The reason I am so thankful for the happy childhood my parents gave me, which at the time I took for granted, is that now I can see how lucky I was to have that bedrock foundation to support me through life's crises as well as its many joys.

Christiane Amanpour is Chief International Correspondent, CNN.

Lisa Aziz

My dad's life story is an amazing one, and
it's what he went through in his journey which
has inspired me in all I do. He was born and
raised in Bangladesh – the eldest son of a judge
– and money was so tight he didn't even have
proper shoes to go to school in. But he was
bright and determined, and did very well at
school. He eventually went overseas to be an
officer cadet at the Royal Naval College in
Dartmouth in Devon where he met my mum,
a local girl who worked in the potteries. They
eloped to marry, and headed east to Karachi
where Dad took up his post in the Pakistan
Navy. They moved house again and again
in order to get better jobs and better
opportunities in life, and I moved with them.

They faced bitter racism and hurdles when they eventually settled in the UK, but it truly did all work out for the best. Having seen a man get through that much adversity and yet retain his sense of humour and community spirit, and want to do so much charity work and help bring on his own Asian community, has left me to this day…awestruck. It was his story which showed me that anything really is possible, and to this day I go to him for all sorts of advice…from jobs to raising my kids. And now he guides my own two children. As far as I'm concerned, he always has the right answer to any problems I may have.

Lisa Aziz is an ITV news presenter and reporter.

DADS, CAKES AND YORKSHIRE PUDDINGS

Ed Balls MP

My father had just one outing in the kitchen when I was growing up. Returning from the hospital the day my little brother was born back in 1973, he declared he would celebrate by cooking a roast beef Sunday lunch for my sister and me. And much to all of our surprise, his Yorkshire puddings not only rose but came clean out of the tin. We all declared it a triumph. He promptly retired on a high, and has dined out on this one triumph ever since – often being unbearably judgemental about the quality of other people's puddings.

The world has moved on – and for me, regular cooking has been both necessary for survival (mine, Yvette's and the family) and also a great way to relax. I enjoy southern American best – Cajun, Mexican, chichi

Californian – and my Yorkshire puddings are regularly passable.

But in recent years I have been branching out into fancy, themed birthday cakes – sometimes using a wonderful *Good Housekeeping* manual of cake patterns, sometimes going it alone and allowing my imagination free rein.

My highpoint so far? A great pirate galleon with liquorice allsorts portholes and Curly Wurly rigging. Closely followed by a 'climbing wall' cake with After Eight bits sticking out as handholds.

More innovative, though slightly less successful, was last year's Coca-Cola can cake... And as for the pink Barbie doll cake the year before, the less said the better.

For interested aficionados, I find Nigella Lawson's buttermilk sponge base very satisfactory – solid and able to bear the weight of icing and trimmings, even when cut and shaped to be the back of a pirate ship. Butter icing is sickly but effective, though I still find food colourings a challenge – trying to get the icing to the right colour without 'E' overload is really hard.

The key to my mind, with birthday cakes, is to consult on the theme but then keep the detailed design a complete surprise until the candles are lit and the children's birthday party is in full swing.

Because even though, as I parade in and see in the eyes of the adults that particular look of respect mixed with horror at my pink monstrosity, I know the children will think it's brilliant – their own special cake, cooked by their mad dad.

Ed Balls MP is Secretary of State for Children, Schools and Families and Member of Parliament for Normanton.

Peter Bazalgette

My father was deserted by his own father in the early 1920s. I'm told my grandfather had been seduced away by all the temptations of that 'roaring' decade. He never saw him again. From the age of two he was raised by his maternal grandfather, a stockjobber by the name of Sanderson. You cannot overestimate the value to a boy of having a father figure. This is underlined by the way in which my father worshipped old Sanderson. That was how he was always referred to in my childhood. I never found out his Christian name. Perhaps he didn't have one.

Sanderson was, by all accounts, profligate, a bit of a boozer and pretty cantankerous. In fact, his outbursts of temper (particularly abuse of slow drivers) were celebrated. But he was generous-hearted enough to give my father and his brother a secure family when they had none. To them he was a god.

At the turn of the century Sanderson had been extremely wealthy. He earned £100,000 in the boom year of 1900 (the equivalent of £7.5 million today), maintaining carriages and a considerable household in Richmond. This had all been dissipated by the 1930s when, in old age, he raised a second family. Indeed, that's why my father left school at 15 to start work. His teachers had wanted him to aim for Classics at Oxbridge. But that was not possible. And, in retrospect, not important either. Old Sanderson and his second wife had already given my father the great start in life that he needed.

Peter Bazalgette is Founder of television production company Bazal, and former Chair of Endemol UK.

Trevor Beattie

You only get the one. You can't yet order them online in bargain blister packs of eight. You get one dad. And he wanders around the place for years and you know not why, really. Then one day, it clicks. You GET him. They say, 'Wait 'til your father gets home,' and one day, he does. You suddenly get the point of your dad. Cherish and recognise that moment. The sooner you experience it, the better. Take it from me, it will never leave you.

One day, I got mine. And from him, a thought which has resonated with me through the years: be yourself. If John Vincent Beattie taught me one simple thing, it was just that. And it's all I've ever really needed. To be proud of who you are, where you're from, what you look like, how you speak. To never, ever, be intimidated or daunted by the status of those you deal with. To be you. And to have people accept you for that.

My dad was a stranger in a strange land, arriving in wartime Birmingham with nothing but an Irish accent as impenetrable as a block of peat and a twinkle in both eyes. He was no fan of authority. Or The System. Or anything that resembled rules, for that matter. And he swept my mum and Birmingham off their collective feet.

He knew who he was. He knew what he wanted. In fact, as a kid, it seemed to me that he simply knew EVERYBODY. And, more importantly, that everybody knew him. He was big. He was Somebody. And then he was gone.

My dad never lived to see me make it in business. (In London! In advertising, for God's sake!) But he'd have recognised the scenario: solus trouble-making Brummie in a world of air-kissing luvvies. Oh yes. His spirit sees me daily through every aspect of business life. At work, we have a large silver 'Jargon Pig' (yes, a piggy bank, kids!). Anyone transgressing, slipping into business jargon (and we do have other phrases for it), must pay an instant fine. Coins in the pig. Clients and agency. It's our reality check.

I've been very very lucky in my career. It has flown me around the world and allowed me to dine with awe-inspiring heroes; from Muhammad Ali to Nelson Mandela. And yet. And yet. I'd give it all up tomorrow and have all those memories erased in exchange for the chance to have dinner with my dad one more time tonight. To remind him that I did and do get him.

You may be even luckier than me. You may still be able to do just that. If so, promise me one thing. That you'll take your dad out tonight. That you'll shut your gob for a change and listen. You might hear him tell you how to become You.

You only get the one. Make sure you GET him. And tell him it was Jack Beattie's idea. It's okay, your dad knows my dad. Everybody does.

Trevor Beattie is an advertising executive at Beattie McGuinness Bungay (BMB), London.

Hilary Benn MP

Growing up with Dad is a swirl of memories. Climbing on to his back as he pretended to be a tree, his pipes and the warm fog of Four Square Yellow tobacco, learning to understand his world while he tried to understand our passion for football and cricket, spending time with him in his office surrounded by paper and gadgets... And conversation – always conversation – about what we were doing, what he was doing, what was happening and why, and what could be done. But I also remember his impish sense of fun.

One Saturday evening, we children had complained once too often that we were bored. About half an hour later the telephone in the living room rang. Dad answered it and his voice become very serious. 'Yes...I see...dangerous?...Of course.' Putting the phone down, he turned to us as we looked on anxiously. 'That was the police. It seems that a dangerous criminal has escaped from the police station down the road. They are warning everyone to be on their guard.' We gulped. Dad suggested that we check that all the doors and windows were locked. We nervously went round the house, keeping up each other's courage as we did so. When we had finished, we peered into the gloom of the back garden, waiting and wondering.

Then, suddenly, we heard a noise that seemed to come from the roof. Our hearts jumped. Could the escaped man really be on our house? What was he going to do? We began to get really worried and crowded around Dad crying out for reassurance. And then, in an instant, his face broke into a twinkly smile as he exclaimed, 'Got you, didn't I?' We screamed in relief and delight, and demanded to know how he had done it. Dad took great pride in showing us how he had made the phone ring and rigged up the string connected to something heavy to make the noise on the roof, which he had tugged away at from the basement. It was some time before we complained about being bored again!

Dad – and Mum – taught us so much, but above all about love, encouragement and family. After all, when the rest has flown, it is these three that sustain us.

Hilary Benn MP is Secretary of State for the Environment, Food and Rural Affairs and MP for Leeds Central.

THE DADDY SHOP
Tony Benn

When I was a Member of Parliament and my children were young, they used to miss me at their great school events and some holidays, so I wrote this story for them.

There were four children whose daddy was always so busy that they decided to go to a Daddy Shop and get a new daddy leaving old daddy in the back of the shop when the new one came out.

The new daddy was wonderful, helping with the housework, always going to sports day and school concerts and plays, helping with their homework and doing everything that their old daddy didn't have time to do.

When Christmas came, their new daddy went to see his own family and as the children sat round the Christmas tree they missed their old daddy and decided to go back to the shop to see if he was still there.

They found him looking very miserable, but when he saw them he leapt up and gave them a huge hug, and they brought him home for Christmas and realised how much they loved him, and he promised to try and be a better daddy.

When I told them this story they all burst into tears, and so did I, and my wife Caroline said that I was never to tell it to them again, because she knew I was transferring my guilt to them, which wasn't fair!

That's why lots of people love old Labour!

Tony Benn is a politician and diarist.

GAFFER: LIFE TO THE FULL

Peter Bennett-Jones

Do you believe in life after death? I never did. It defies logic, obviously. To me dying was the final act of living, after which, oblivion. The living are left with a person-sized gap in their lives, mourn the loss and there it ends. Until, that is, the recent death of my darling dad. He lives on.

The coastal edge of the Isle of Anglesey is a blustery, chilly place in February. Grey is the prevailing colour – sea, sky, pebble-dash houses, chapels. The outwardly dilapidated Paran Methodist Chapel on High Street, Rhosneigr, is as slate, slab grey as you get. Once inside, however, the atmosphere transforms, especially when the sturdy pews are packed shoulder to shoulder by friends and family of a much loved man who they had congre-gated to remember and honour, a man cremated earlier that day in the tradition established by one of his heroes, the great fellow Welshman Dr William Price. My adorable dad, known to one and all as Gaffer.

It was a scene which Dylan Thomas would have relished. A dapper minister presiding over a respectful but lustily voiced predominantly Welsh crowd, determined to see this popular old boy off in style. They raised the roof with 'Bread of Heaven'.

The life we were gathered to celebrate was a magnificently full one. A farmer's boy who had won the county scholarship, graduated as a doctor with double first class honours, served in the RAMC in the Burma campaign, administered extraordinary diagnostic skills in the newly formed NHS for decades, raised a family while pursuing a host of interests.

I had agreed to deliver one of two eulogies. The first, given by cousin Wynn, contained an extraordinarily mature and moving passage quoted from a letter home, sent by the young officer from the Far East during the Second World War. Written to his recently bereaved and widowed young sister, it offered the following support for the fledgling Wynn, his nephew, 'Wynn will never know what a giant of a man his father was: but there is not one of us who will refuse to sacrifice all that is in our power to make it up to him as best we can. Between us we must and shall make it a sacred duty to mould his character so that the life in store for him will be as full of good purposes as his father's.' Wynn choked as he confirmed that Dad had been as good as his word.

My task was simpler. I adored my dad and had little trouble in listing his many virtues: loyalty, sensitivity, patriotism, curiosity, professionalism, generosity, modesty, brilliance, courtesy, humour. In doing so I experienced a strange sensation. I was struck almost physically by his presence after death, by his power and influence. I realised as I stood in the wooden pulpit in this modest chapel that his life was not over – he was part of the future as well as the past. He would govern the direction of my life for years to come – a talisman to lead one towards a set of admirable values. I realised that the presence of those who have lived cannot be expunged, cannot be finally burnt or buried – they are part of our future as well as our history.

By focussing on my father's life and achievements and on his humanity, his spirit became an almost tangible force. My life felt enriched in this moment of remembrance – a sadness that his physical presence was gone for ever but happiness that he remained an indelible paternal force for good.

I ended my eulogy with a recent anecdote that encapsulated this special man. A couple of weeks earlier I was with my mother and sister, who were nursing him brilliantly in his final, cancer-ridden days. He was dozing, slightly drugged. I offered the girls a glass of restorative champagne to raise the spirits. I tapped Dad on the shoulder and politely asked if he would like half a glass of bubbly. He awoke. He smiled. He paused for thought. He said deliberately, 'Peter, dear boy, you should know now that I have never really liked...[longer pause]...the word half. Fill it to the brim!' It was his last proper drink! He died living life to the full and he lives on.

Peter Bennett-Jones, agent and producer, is Chairman of Tiger Aspect Productions and of Comic Relief.

Sanjeev Bhaskar

Fatherhood. Two years in and it continues to be the most exhilarating experience of my life. The highest highs and the lowest lows. From anxiety about your child's wellbeing that threatens to consume your very soul, to the smallest approbation via a smile or a hug that makes you glow inside like a thousand suns. As fathers we are divorced from the physical aspects of pregnancy (with immense gratitude towards the mothers!) and thus our physical relationship begins a good nine months after them. I spent those nine months hoping that I would be up to the task of being a dad. Could I possibly be worthy enough to guide and protect the small piece of perfection, pure and unsullied, that was hurtling in my direction?

Twenty-four months later and addled with tiredness, the constant spectre of some bug or the other hanging round like an unwanted groupie, and consciously avoiding any acknowledgement of the ageing process, what's really changed? Well, it becomes harder to remember that the cause of all this consternation is essentially still that small piece of perfection that you awaited with such bated breath, such a short time before. Your little unsullied treasure now has a will and a voice and an inconvenience that at times can seem personally directed at you. And though they're already noisy, smelly, stubborn, tiny people, they are still unblemished by spite, cynicism and prejudice.

WE dream of our children bringing us glory by making their mark on the world in some positive way, perhaps scoring the winning goal in the cup final, mentioning us in their Oscar speech or inventing some wonder drug. Maybe the best thing we can do is to make sure that they are a slight improvement on us. Surely then, the human race would be heading in the right direction.

The most profound moment for me thus far? Not the first smile, the first laugh, the first word, although undoubtedly amazing. It was when on hearing thunder for the first time, my happy little boy looked anxiously around, spotted me and crawled quickly into my lap. I was awestruck. I had been accorded the honour of his total trust. He trusted that I would keep him safe from the rumbles of the universe. So? Am I worthy enough to guide and protect this small piece of perfection? I don't know, but tomorrow I'm going to try a little bit harder than I did today to be so.

Sanjeev Bhaskar is a comedian, actor and author.

John Bird

My dad taught me one principle: never beat a woman. Unfortunately, he taught me that lesson by leading by counter-example. However, I'll be proud if, at the end of my life, it can be said that I stopped the reproduction of violence against women in the family. Today I have five children. I am a dad and a granddad. My younger children are less than two years old, which is great because that means that I have a fresh chance to improve my parenting skills. Today, I am much more aware of my role, of the importance I will have in my children's life, and therefore I am working harder at being a proper dad than before. It is hard work, but it is so rewarding.

Children should be the priority of all dads and sometimes we should also parent children who unfortunately do not get the chance of having parents. With care for others at the centre of any policy, that would make a much better society.

John Bird is Founder and Editor-in-Chief of The Big Issue.

David Blunkett MP

The death of my father, when I was 12 years old, was more than simply the loss of a parent, of a loved one, of someone I cared deeply about.

It was the loss of a friend. Because I was an only child (effectively, because my older half-sister Doreen had already left home when I was born), and because I spent the whole of my years from the age of four at boarding school (compulsory in those days), my dad was my friend and mentor during the holidays. Mum looked after the home and ensured food was on the table and provided warmth and comfort. Dad was the one I played with, I walked with, I spent time listening to.

His formal education had been limited, but his general knowledge was prodigious. He would hammer into me facts about capital cities across the world – and how they are related to each other – which I am sure stimulated my own thinking and interest in current affairs.

The long walks that we took together – and which resulted in my mum grumbling about the blisters on my feet and how tired out I often was – were like the early trips to sit on the wall behind the goal, the kop end of Hillsborough, the home of my beloved Sheffield Wednesday, memories never to be forgotten.

So when I visited him on numerous occasions in what was then the Sheffield Royal Infirmary, smelling, feeling, hurting with him after the horrendous accident which, four weeks on, led to his death, I carried and still do an imprint of a role model of courage, of the critical importance of fatherhood. His belief that I could do whatever it was that I thought possible; his unswerving willingness to let me take risks, to play as other boys played and, yes, to split my head open at the age of four, having fallen off the bike which had run down the hill with me still on it!

That is why it is so important that in every child's life there is a mum and a dad – whether at a distance or in the same home – caring, loving and giving a variety of experiences.

It is the two halves of the brain, the two halves of all of us that make it possible to be a rounded human being. Where there is no birth father, hopefully there will be a substitute – someone who cares and feels and reflects in just the same way. Which is why, although we cannot restore the old industrial apprenticeships of the past, we can recapture some of the value that they offered – again to mentor, to metaphorically clip an ear, to tell stories and to instil that respect for others. Strength in manhood through thoughtfulness, kindness and care.

A functioning society needs us to learn the lessons of the past and to apply them to the possibilities of the future. And this is why, if we can avoid doing so, we should never lose contact with those who provide that stability, that security and that perspective on life.

David Blunkett MP is a former Cabinet Minister, and has been Member of Parliament for Sheffield Brightside since 1987.

Sir Richard Branson

When I was seven, I noticed my dad putting his loose change from his pocket in the top cabinet drawer. Well, we lived next to a sweet shop and one day I climbed on a stool and took a handful of his change and went around to the shop. A large pile of sweets grew on the counter but before I could pick them up, Mrs Arnell, who knew I only got a very small amount of pocket-money, got on the phone and called my dad around.

When he arrived, he looked Mrs Arnell straight in the eye: 'Mrs Arnell, how dare you accuse my son of stealing.' He picked up the sweets, left the shop holding my hand, dumped the sweets in the bin, and never said

anything to me about it. He didn't need to.
I never went near his drawer again!

Richard Branson is an entrepreneur and Founder of Virgin, now an international brand with around 200 companies in over 30 countries.

Christopher Brookmyre

So it's 31 October 2001. I'm living with my wife and 18-month-old son in Bridge of Don, in a rented house in a quiet, modern cul-de-sac. Jack is a bit young for the dressing-up thing, but, for once, I am ready for Hallowe'en. After years of the urban tenement guising experience – opening your door to two teenagers with one ten-bob false face from Tesco's between them and the plastic bag it came in held out to you with a vague air of threat – I realise the effort being put in by the local weans deserves to be met with appropriate confectionery recognition.

I'm starting to get to know the neighbours, though ironically what broke the ice and got us all talking was the local press and radio indulging in a bit of postured civic outrage at my cruel (but accurate) depiction of Aberdeen in a recent novel. I figure providing a good-humoured and bounteous trick-or-treating destination should go a long way towards dispelling notions that the monsters of my written imagination lurk only one thin layer beneath the derma.

It's about seven. There are various multi-bags of sweeties by the door, as well as monkey nuts and apples by way of tradition and to placate any dental-conscious parents. I've got Jack's bath running, nearly ready. My wife should have been home a while back, but it's nothing unusual. She'll be in any minute. I pick up Jack and carry him to the bathroom, where his changing mat is laid out on the floor. As I approach it, a concerned look appears on Jack's face, the only warning I get before he warps the fabric of space-time TARDIS-style by spewing up a volume of boak far in excess of his own bodyweight. He also covers my face, chest, trousers, socks, the spray-back effect spattering him from chin to foot also. Despite this, he looks utterly unperturbed by the experience. It is perhaps a recall of this infant ability that extreme heavy drinkers are able to tap into later in life, in executing what Billy Connolly called 'the casual vomit'.

At this point, the doorbell rings. I can hear their voices, children's giggles, the lower tones of adults escorting them. I am literally dripping spew as I undress Jack, figuring I'll bathe him, stick a fresh nappy on him and sit him in a bouncer-seat next to the bath while I have a shower.

The doorbell rings again.

The lights are on, the car is in the driveway. They think I'm blanking them.

I giggle. Sudden third-person perspective upon the absurdity is what gets you through at such times. This is funny. The doorbell rings again. My T-shirt is clinging and I can feel bits of partially digested bean nestling in my chest hair. I briefly entertain the notion of running down and answering it as I am.

'Greetings,' I'd say. 'We're just about to go out guising ourselves: I'm Captain Vomit and Jack's going to be Diarrhoea Boy. He's up in the bathroom just now, working on his outfit.'

Maybe not. I'm peeling off my clothes, letting them squelch into the puddle at my feet as I hear my neighbours pointing out the rank hypocrisy of this rude Glaswegian who had the cheek to slag Aberdonians for their lack of hospitality.

Forget the soft-focus moments and the Disney version of fatherhood. True dads know this kind of story isn't just the real stuff, it's the good stuff.

Christopher Brookmyre is the author of 11 novels, including Quite Ugly One Morning *and* Attack of the Unsinkable Rubber Ducks.

Bill Bryson

My father, when behind the wheel, was more or less permanently lost. Most of the time he was just kind of lost, but whenever we got near something we were intent on seeing, he would become seriously lost. Generally it would take him about an hour to realise that he had gone from the first stage to the second. All during that time, as he blundered through some unfamiliar city, making sudden and unpredictable turns, getting honked at for going the wrong way down one-way streets or for hesitating in the middle of busy intersections, my mother would mildly suggest that perhaps we should pull over and ask directions. But my father would pretend not to hear her and would

press on in that semi-obsessional state
that tends to overcome fathers when
things aren't going well.

Eventually, after driving the wrong way down
the same one-way street so many times that
merchants were beginning to come and watch
from their doorways, Dad would stop the car
and gravely announce, 'Well, I think we
should ask directions,' in a tone suggesting
that this had been his desire all along.

He was a great dad. I miss him a lot.

Bill Bryson is a bestselling author and broadcaster.

LOVING FATHER
Michael Cashman MEP

Life wasn't easy in the 1950s for a family that lived and worked in the heart of the docklands in London's East End, and I had a really difficult relationship with my father. Maybe it was partly due to being brought up in a tough working-class family, and also because I became an actor at such a young age, when I was 12 years old.

As a young kid, my dad was the source of great fun to me. When he was drunk, the fun was at its best. And he did like to drink. But then my relationship changed with him. Distance grew between us for many reasons, not the least being his relationship with my mum. In the arguments and the fights, I always took her side. Over the years I convinced myself that there was no love between us. Then in the mid-1980s I went through therapy, and I made a staggering discovery. I remember how in one of the sessions I had to talk about what I did as a child during the day. One of the things I described was that when I was at home from school for dinner (lunch) and my dad was there, I would let down the tyres on his bike.

'Why do you do that?' I was asked.

I remember vividly the next exchange between us.

''Cos I don't want him to go back to work.'

'Why?'

'Because I love him.'

'And does your daddy love you?'

'I don't know,' I responded, and I broke down and sobbed.

The revelation was life changing.

That had been the source of my dislike for my father. I just didn't know whether he loved me.

Over the next ten years we grew closer, and then one day, after a TV programme I had made on homophobia had been transmitted, he phoned me at home. 'I'm proud of you, son. Proud of you,' then he stuttered and fell silent.

'What's wrong?' I asked.

After a pause he replied, 'And I love you.'

The sense of real belonging that I felt then, and still feel, can never be properly described.

I was so lucky to have found the truth of the relationship that we had, so fortunate to have had the love of my dad. And as a working-class man, so fortunate to have heard him say it.

Michael Cashman MEP is a former actor, and has been Member of the European Parliament for the West Midlands since 1999.

Sebastian Coe

My parents became a little curious, and perhaps a little nervous, when they noticed their 12-year-old son had started spending an increasing amount of time, evenings and mornings, at the local athletics club and wanted to know more about what was going on...

My father's background was in road cycling, and given the forensic nature of his engineer's mind, what started out as a parental interest of relatively marginal concern, turned into something more hands-on and structured, as he absorbed everything about the sport of athletics.

After a year of watching, he decided he could coach me better. So, from when I was 13 to 14 years of age, my father became my first and last serious coach until I was 34 years old, when I retired.

He navigated me through the early years, nurturing a young talent into an international athlete, the toughest years in coaching, through two Olympic Games and world records.

The memory that will always live with me was when he made me realise how far down the road he was thinking… When I was still shy of my fourteenth birthday, he took me aside at the end of a rain-soaked training session and said, 'I don't want you to be too surprised by this, but you will be going to the Olympic Games.' It was something that I did not fully take on board at the time. It took me a few more years before that observation properly sank in.

My father was an unflinching believer in the talent he saw, and as a result I believe that it is absolutely crucial in the early days that a coach can paint pictures for their charges.

My father also quickly understood the quirky nature of handling athletes. He recognised what the best coaches know in dealing with athletes, that less is sometimes more, and that understanding the person you are working with is as important as mastering the demands of the event. Psychology and physiology in equal parts.

I trusted him implicitly and by dint of hard work and intellectual rigour, he became one of the foremost thinkers in the art and science of middle-distance training. We are great friends.

I think his only regret was that we never won the Tour de France!

Sebastian Coe is a former top athlete, currently Chairman of the London Organising Committee of the Olympic Games and Paralympic Games.

TEN IMPORTANT THINGS I LEARNED FROM MY DAD

Andrew Collins

1. It is important to beat the traffic. This involves getting up unusually early and setting off on car journeys before everybody else does.

2. There is no word you cannot insert into the phrase, 'I'll _____ you in a minute.' In other words, if Dad calls you in from the garage because Mum has the dinner on the table, and you say you'll be another five minutes because you've got one last torpedo tube to attach to your Airfix model of the Graf Spee battle cruiser, he will say, with mock gravity, 'I'll Graf Spee you in a minute.' Equally, if you have torn your new trousers and you blame it on your brother Simon, he'll say, 'I'll Simon you in a minute.' See how it works.

3. Never throw out old trainers, or old shirts, or old socks, even old pants, as they'll do for the garden.

4. In arguments always defer to Mum. Though this may seem like an overly submissive kind of marital surrender, it's actually more about saving up your Joker, so that when you do disagree, or gainsay, or differ, in a future argument, it will have that much more impact.

5. Clean your plate. I have almost reached the age my dad was when I was 18 and about to leave home, and I can honestly say that this is the most profound lesson he passed on to me. I would rather make myself sick than leave food on a plate, whether at home or in the finest restaurants of London. If there is bread to mop up the juice, all the better.

6. Insure everything. Dad worked in insurance all of his working life, and as far as I can see, this is why he remains so laid-back. As long as it's insured, there's no need to get into a flap if it is damaged or nicked.

7. Driving prevents car sickness. If only I'd been able to drive the family to North Wales like he did, perhaps I would never have been sick out of the window – or in the plastic potty Mum and Dad kept in the back on long journeys – halfway up the A5 to Shrewsbury.

8. Tony Hancock is the greatest comedian that ever lived. There is something about the cultural inheritance that passes between father and son that cannot be matched, especially in terms of comedy. I could sit down right now with my dad and watch an old Hancock, or *Monty Python and the Holy Grail*, or *Blazing Saddles*, or listen to one of Peter Sellers' comedy songs. Dads know their comedy.

9. Be nice to people. It disarms horrible people, and encourages other nice people to be nice to you. Expressing love was not something in my dad's genetic make-up when I was growing up. We did not hug until the twenty-first century. But he was always nice.

10. Vote Conservative. Actually, I choose to ignore this.

Andrew Collins is an author, scriptwriter and broadcaster.

Mary Contini

Perched high in the front seat of my father's Volkswagen van, I could see far into the distance. I clung on tightly to the dashboard as the van wound its way down the East Lothian coast to Eyemouth. It was very early, and, in the summer northern light, the sea on our left sparkled.

Daddy sucked on his pipe which balanced unlit from the side of his mouth. He was quiet, deep in thought. He had finished work at 2 a.m. that morning, and now we were off to the fish market to buy the fish for the weekend.

In those days, food miles, local sourcing and organics were unheard of. There was no choice for my father but to buy the fish direct from the fishermen, the potatoes from the farm and the milk from the local dairy. His ice cream and fish and chip business thrived on wonderful fresh local produce. In the summer, hoards of holiday-makers and day-trippers from Glasgow and Edinburgh created a constant queue and, as far as I can remember, they were endless, beautiful sunny days.

Arriving at the harbour, Daddy lifted me down from the van and, leaving me to follow, walked towards the market. The boats were lined up along the pier, jostling against each other, ropes and chains clunking noisily. The huge shed to the left was brimming full of boxes of all kinds of fish, all sparkling and fresh, wriggling and squirming, tails flapping in desperation to return to the sea. Blue lobsters and scarlet crabs snapped at each other through netted pots. Fishermen shouted to each other, hands flying as deals were done.

My father's uproarious laugh rang out over the crowd and fishermen turned to slap his back, shake his hand and greet him with obvious affection. I was handed a Scottish 'bridie' from one of the men, and I chewed on it as I followed my dad around as he picked up the fish, selected his choice and, pulling a wad of notes from his back pocket, exchanged cash and shook on the deal. Afterwards I stood outside the pub while he downed a pint of beer, then, pink-cheeked, me from the warming sun, Dad from the beer, we headed back to the van.

On the way home my father was quiet again, contemplating the day ahead. He would have to gut and fillet the fish till noon, clean and chip two sacks of potatoes, then stand in the shop till 12 at night frying up the very best fish and chips.

As I grew up he never spoke to me about business, but by example taught me to work hard, be honest and fair, and appreciate the suppliers, staff and customers with equal respect and humour. Years later when I told my father I wanted to marry Philip, a young Italian boy from the delicatessen, Valvona & Crolla, he was not impressed.

'You'll end up behind the counter!' was his assessment of my choice.

He was right. I did, but at least he had prepared me from a very early age for how to do business!

Mary Contini is Director of Valvona & Crolla Ltd, and author of Dear Francesca *and* Dear Olivia.

Ronnie Corbett

I hope my mother is going to read this in heaven…as I could write about her with as much love and feeling as I now write about my dad.

What a giver he was, what a worker, and what an example he set to us all. Most of his life was spent night baking, returning home about eleven in the morning, yet he still had the energy to take us walking, or to see a military parade, or to our weekly swim at Warrender Baths… Even a few holes of golf, and a lesson or two on the Braid Hills, south of Edinburgh.

He had so much time for everybody…and was devoted to the church, his church, College Street Church in Edinburgh. An elder of the church, a member of the choir, morning service and evening service, he was a great attender. On the odd Sunday when he had to go to the bakery, near Orwell Terrace, on his own for the sponging, I think it was called – some important part of the dough process, with natural yeast – he would take me with him, and I remember it all like a fairytale. This huge empty bakehouse, with only him and me there. I was allowed the freedom to roam. One of the bakehouse cats had always had kittens, and the family would be safely housed in jute sacking, in an old dried fruit tub in the loft. It was an Aladdin's cave, that loft, raisins, sultanas, dates, muscatels, glacé cherries, marzipans – all for the nibbling, what a treat.

He has left me so many, many examples: nothing was ever hammered home, he just set them all by his own personal effort and commitment to life. My God, I was a lucky boy.

Ronnie Corbett is an actor and comedian.

Jon Culshaw

My dad, James Culshaw, has always been the most reassuring, calm presence that we have known. With an ever-present kindness, he has a natural ability to turn any tense, worrying or complex situation into something disarmingly simple, with just a few logical, calm words.

He has been admired for his talent as a craftsman and joiner throughout his life. I remember looking around inside our family home and realising that all of it had been hand-built over the years by Dad in his shed in the back garden. Wardrobes, cupboards, tables, window ledges, doors, sheds, stair banisters, even teapot stands – Dad had made them all in his shed.

He still does today, age 89! The trusty shed is as it ever was. A workbench with all kinds of tools, lawnmowers and practical objects, all put in their correct order. It remains the much-loved place where my dad works. Stepping in there today, I'm instantly transported back to my earliest childhood memories by the aroma of wood shavings.

My dad served in the Second World War with the Royal Engineers, and occasionally he tells me some of his experiences from that time. One that sticks in my mind is the moving story of my dad and two friends from his regiment who, one typical day, were given the task of defusing two unexploded bombs, work they often had to undertake. After some conferring, the officer in charge decided to send the two friends to one site and my dad to the other, to begin the job.

Tragically, shortly afterwards there was a huge explosion, claiming the lives of his two friends. The severity of the blast had left them almost impossible to identify. I can't imagine how he coped with the devastation of losing his mates in this way, and the haunting knowledge that this could easily have been his own fate, had chance simply played out the opposite way.

My admiration and respect for soldiers like my dad is only exceeded by my love for him. Just imagine, day after day, defusing bombs, wondering if this was the moment your luck might run out. High stakes like that I find profoundly sobering and humbling to contemplate. Dad simply sums it up with his typical humility and calm modesty, saying, 'You had to get on with it.' No wonder they say those in our armed forces are our finest.

I manage to get back home to Lancashire every few weeks to visit my family and old friends. It's always a treasured experience. I love it, especially in the mornings when my dad serves up a plateful of his trademark hot buttered toast made on my mum's 1950s' flame grill, together with a steaming cup of coffee in his special mug with the Clangers on it. For me, it's one of those simple joys in life, when you can't help feeling a great sense of contentment and of all being well with the world.

Jon Culshaw is an impressionist and comedian.

Richard Curtis

My dad died last summer, and it's probably no coincidence that I find myself quoting him more and more. It's strange, as he must have said a million things to me but certain of them have just stuck, probably because they were in some ways especially true of him and his life.

He passed them on to me, so I pass a few on to you. At his most pessimistic, he used to say, 'A problem is a problem because it can't be resolved.' I'm an instinctive optimist and I've always found that very helpful – sometimes there just is no solution, and it's time to move on. A detailed little nugget of his was, 'Never ask a question you don't already know the answer to.' I don't think he meant that for the whole of life, but it is a good business hint: if you really know what you want to happen, don't ask everyone their opinions and then spend the next weeks or years wishing you'd just said what you wanted.

Most important – and probably the cornerstone of my life – was his catchphrase, 'You can't be happier than happy'. I think of that every day. If you're happy, be happy with the fact you're happy, don't think, 'Well, yes, it's a good film, but I could have been in a comfier cinema with a bigger tub of popcorn, sitting between Kate Moss and Cheryl Cole.'

And then sometimes Dad was more specific. I remember I'd been going through a particularly lean period with girlfriends, for about four lonely years, and finally Dad took me into his study, and said that he had some advice that he felt he must share with me, which might get me out of trouble. I went in, expecting a long and careful lecture. Instead of which, Dad just turned to me and said, 'The answer to your problem, son, is nurses.' Apparently, in Sydney in the 1940s, nurses were the only ones comfortable with taking their clothes off for fun – and Dad had taken full advantage of it. Unexpectedly, even that turned out to be excellent advice during the wonderful summer of 1988.

I'm now busy passing on my dad's advice to my children. They know you can't be happier than happy, they know sometimes problems can't be resolved. But can anyone tell me whether the nurses thing is still true in 2008?

Richard Curtis is a writer, director and producer, best known for films such as Four Weddings and a Funeral *and* Notting Hill, *and TV programmes,* The Vicar of Dibley *and* Blackadder.

Paul Dacre

One of my most vivid memories of my dad, who was also a journalist, is being taken on my first visit to our local public library, in Arnos Grove, a North London suburb. I was about ten and he chose three novels for me by Conan Doyle, H. Rider Haggard and C. S. Forester. They were all, in their way, about the days when Britain ruled the world and, I'm afraid, terribly politically incorrect by today's standards. They were also electrifyingly exciting for a young boy in the fifties, and from that day on I became an insatiable reader, visiting the library every week.

When my dad was four, his father, who was a carpenter, was killed in a building site accident. At 14, my dad left school, joined a local newspaper and was on Fleet Street by the age of 22. More than anything, he loved words and the creative process, writing TV scripts in his spare time and composing songs, of which his best-known was sung by Bing Crosby.

In his thirties, he became New York correspondent (a post I was later to hold) of the *Sunday Express*, which in those days was a great paper with a circulation of nearly five million – compared to 600,000 today. Such was the shortage of space in our rented Manhattan home that I had to share my bedroom with the ticker-tape telex machine that was directly linked to London. Because of the time difference, it would often clatter to life in the early hours with 'File soonest...' requests from the foreign desk on a fast-breaking story. Nothing could have been more exciting for a young boy fascinated by journalism than watching his father telexing over a story with seconds to spare to meet a deadline.

I had four brothers so you can imagine that we were all somewhat competitive. As he worked very late, Sunday was the only day we saw our father. If he'd got a piece in that week's paper he was a happy man. Conversely, if his article had been killed by the then editor – the tyrannical and legendary John Junor – he was in a black mood. Either way, Sunday lunches would be dominated by talk analysing that day's paper. Who had written the best intro? What was the most striking picture? Was the overall balance of the paper right?

When we were tardy in doing our homework, my father's favourite saying to us boys was, 'Procrastination is the thief of time…' It's advice that I have singularly failed to live up to because, like most journalists, I leave everything to the last minute. My father, however, did teach me a passion for words. Even today, after being an editor for nearly 18 years – and our newspapers' computer systems seem a million years away from that New York telex machine – I still get an enormous thrill from a beautiful piece of writing.

Paul Dacre is Editor of the Daily Mail, *and Editor-in-Chief of Associated Newspapers.*

FATHERHOOD'S FINE. IT'S HAVING KIDS THAT KILLS YOU.

(An extract from a stand-up routine)

Ben Elton

Nothing prepares you for how tired you're going to be when you have small kids. I'm middle-aged, I've got three of them. It's hell. Don't let anyone pretend it isn't. I refuse to buy into this modern touchy-feely bollocks and pretend it's all wonderful; yes, you love them, yes, you'd die for them, but it's still unmitigated hell!

People ask me why I went on tour again after ten years – why do you think? To get a few nights away from the little bastards, that's why! I'll tell you what, when you've got three small kids, you do miss the soft gentle hum of a hotel mini-bar.

What about all these old blokes having second families, Rod Stewart, Michael Douglas...why do they do it?

It's exhausting…and I'll tell you another thing, having kids ruins your sex life, and it's not easy to get it back once it's gone. My wife and I ended up having to use those video sex aids to help us get things going again. If we put on *Postman Pat* we might get five minutes to have a shag!

And how's Rod going to manage the school morning? There is no hell like the school morning, nothing on earth prepares you for it. Ninety minutes of pure unadulterated hell. Trying to get the little so-and-so's out of bed, get them washed, get them de-nitted, get them filled full of sugar-coated crap masquerading as food, put their underpants back on the right way round, get their homework packed up…get 'em in the car…while all the time they're dragging their feet, going back in time, becoming obsessed with a lost pebble which they haven't given a thought to for three months, but is now suddenly more precious than the koh-i-noor. It's hell, and it happens every day!

I saw this child psychologist on *Richard and Judy*. She said you mustn't get angry. Oh no, you mustn't get angry because kids live in the now. That's right, they have no sense of urgency. They're not trying to make you angry; it's just that they live in the now. No, it's because they're complete bastards that's why! Your kids...my kids...all of 'em.

It's hell. Seven-thirty in the morning trying to fill in a homework book with the pen that doesn't work? What is it about the pen that doesn't work?! I've got this pen in my house, it doesn't work and I can't get rid of it! It's like a boomerang; I throw it away, it comes back. All the pens that do work evaporate, they dissolve on the way back from WH Smith. But the pen that doesn't work will never leave the house; it's always there – by the phone, by the homework – anywhere I need a pen, there it is.

The pressure on parents these days is outrageous. The other night my wife and I were up all night, jibbering with nervous tension, consumed with paranoia...because we'd been entrusted with the class hamster for the evening! I work hard...I pay my tax...I'm entitled to some leisure time. I should not have the well-being of a much-loved rodent arbitrarily thrust upon me, it's not fair. We were up all night, me and her, listening to its little pulse, checking its little heartbeat, thinking, 'Please don't die! Please don't let us be the family that killed the class hamster!' In the morning I'm cleaning its straw, picking the shit out with a microscope and tweezers, because we don't want to be the dirty family, do we? We don't want to be the family that took the hamster back to school with shit in its straw. So eventually I'm carrying this buffed, cleaned and blow-dried hamster in cotton-wool litter towards the Ford people mover.

One of my kids says, 'We need them little silver foil cups they put Mr Kipling cakes in…we need the little silver dishes for our collages!'

I say, 'Well we haven't got any,' and suddenly the kid's crying like I've murdered his dog.

'We've got to have 'em! We've got to have 'em, everyone else will have 'em!'

So I've got to drive to the Esso station, buy a tray of Kipling cakes, throw the cakes out the window, come home, wash up the little trays…

My wife says, 'Have you got the bag of cardboard we've been collecting for craft?' Yes, I've got the bag of cardboard we've been collecting for craft, because – let's face it – I've got nothing else to do with my life other than empty out the last cornflakes from the bottom of the box and then carefully flatten it out, and try to avoid getting any egg on the egg box! I don't want to collect cardboard. I just want to go to school and say, there's twenty quid, please buy some cardboard!

So I've got the hamster...I've got the Mr Kipling trays. I've got the cardboard. I go to school. 'There you are Miss Whatsit, there's your bag of cardboard.'

She looks in it; she says, 'Thank you Mr Elton but we don't take toilet rolls.' I say, 'But that's the best bit, that's your telescope that is...you can't do without toilet rolls – they're the basis of your submarine, your howitzer, your space rocket...you've got to have toilet rolls!'

And she says, 'We don't take toilet rolls, Mr Elton. It's policy.' She makes me feel like a pervert...makes me feel like I'm trying to thrust my whiffy toilet rolls on five-year-old kids.

Everything about kids drives you mad. And nights are worse than mornings! You can't get them down, you can't get them up! The other night, we finally got them down – not *put* them down – although it does cross my mind sometimes...We'd bathed them, read them five stories, and then read them another five stories, brushed their teeth, brushed their teeth again after the toast frenzy because they didn't eat their tea, found the lost teddy bear...got them into bed...dealt with the littlest one's physical compulsion to revisit us 15 times after the lights have gone out – down he comes, 'go to bed', up he goes...down he comes, 'go to bed', up he goes... down he comes...Finally the war of attrition is won and he collapses asleep on the stairs! I have to carry him up. She says, 'Are you taking him up?', which translates as 'I'm not taking him up mate'. So I take him up and put him in his bed under his little Thomas the Tank duvet, and just as he rolls over he smiles and says, 'I love you Dadda.' A little sleepy smile and 'I love you Dadda'. That's how they do it, you know. That's how they survive! They push you and push you until you're at the very point where you're going to throw them out the window, and then they gurgle and say, 'I love you Dadda,' and they're safe for another day!

So I'm finally back downstairs...It's eight-thirty, a precious bit of adult time, and with shaking hand I'm trying to get the corkscrew into the cork, because we know we've got to drink fast because we need to be in bed by nine, because it's all going to start again tomorrow.

So we're just relaxing, having a nice little drinky; we're finished, exhausted, we have no more left to give…

My wife says, 'Oh no! I never checked the front flap of her school bag when we did the homework, I never checked the front flap!'

So I go and get it…with trepidation I open it… Out comes the note…the note. 'Dear Parents, could you kindly send your child to school tomorrow dressed…as an Elizabethan.'

Ben Elton is a writer and comedian.

Sir Alex Ferguson

Do you know one of the great disciplines my father instilled in me was timekeeping? Every morning, around 6.15 a.m., my brother and I would get the old shake of the foot from my dad; no words were needed, the shake told us it was time to get up and go to work. After a few minutes' extra respite from the exposure to those awful cold Glasgow mornings, we'd hear those well-used words, 'Are those two up yet?', followed by the thunder of his feet making their way up to our bedroom. Did we move? You bet we did, like greyhounds out of a trap, grabbing at anything resembling clothes. Goodness, that was the hardest bit of the day and yet the most rewarding; this simple discipline of my dad's regarding timekeeping has stayed with me all my life. I was never late for work in six years as a toolmaker and I have tried to instil this in my own sons, as basically to some degree you are what your parents want you to be. But as you grow into adulthood you develop your own character and personality, and I have noticed this clearly with my own sons.

Sir Alex Ferguson is a former football player, currently Manager of Manchester United football club.

DAD
Ben Fogle

'Gggggrrrrrrrrrrrrrrrrrrrrrrrrrrrrrrrrrrrrrrrrrrr'

I lay on the ground, curled in the foetal position as the grizzly bear growled and swiped at me with its hairy paw.

'Gggggrrrrrrrrrrrrrrrrrrrrrrrrrrrr'

I was just 12, in the midst of an attack by one of the world's most dangerous animals, and I was giggling uncontrollably. Guffawing. Laughing so much it hurt.

I was in Hyde Park, in central London, and the grizzly was in fact *Dad* with an oven glove.

He had taken my best friend Toby and I for 'bear attack' training classes. While all our other friends were busy playing cricket and football, *my* dad was teaching us how to survive a potential grizzly bear attack.

He was training us for a summer camping trip we had planned across Canada's Algonquin Park, in my grandfather's hand-made cedar Canadian canoe.

We spent ten days in the wilderness. It was the best holiday of my life. Just the three of us. Me, Toby and *Dad*.

Dad paddled, fished, and cooked. We dived for fresh-water mussels and crayfish. We saw magnificent moose and industrious beavers. We carried the canoe around waterfalls, and picked leeches from our legs. Dad taught us how to be men.

We never did see a grizzly bear, but I've never forgotten that sunny, summer's afternoon in Hyde Park, giggling and thinking how much I loved *my* dad.

Ben Fogle is an adventurer and television presenter. His father is Bruce Fogle.

Bruce Fogle

During the 60-plus years that I knew him, I never once had a truly meaningful conversation with my father. After I'd become an adult I tried to have one, but never got anywhere.

Throughout his life my dad was there but not there. It was as if he were background noise – a strapping physical presence, always around, always doing stuff, but not proactively involved with his children. By profession he was a florist, but to me he was our resident builder, the fix-it man, muscle when I needed someone with more strength than I had, the provider, the man always with cash in his pocket, the guy who gave me corsages to give to girls when I first started dating. He was a quiet person, compellingly strong and physically robust, someone with great presence but not given to words and certainly not to expressions of emotion.

After I married and had kids of my own, my family lived above my veterinary clinic. That bit of serendipity meant I saw my kids, Emily, Ben and Tamara, more frequently than some dads do. I was there when they were sick in bed or at home during term breaks. I was around when they experienced the jubilations and torments of growing up.

My wife Julia, not unlike my own nonagenarian mother, is an instinctively 'maternal' mother and the kids always did, and still do, thrive on her inherent physical and emotional warmth. Unconsciously, a father brings uniquely different qualities to what a mother brings to parenting. As a dad my natural activities when the kids were young were also physical, but in a completely different way. I hung them upside down between my legs. I ran with them bobbing errantly on my shoulders, clinging to my hair. I swung them in circles by their arms and legs. I played hide and seek with them. Fathers rouse kids. We intuitively stir their physical sensations. Later, when their emotions were in turmoil, I tended to get dispassionate. I felt more comfortable talking them through what was happening, rather than just enveloping them in a warm, protective fug. I'm sure this too is innate in men. We bring different values to parenting but they're just as vital. Kids who miss out on the different activities and responses that mothers and fathers instinctively bring to parenting are disadvantaged from birth.

By today's standards, the role my dad played in my life would probably be frowned upon. He died when he was 97 and at his funeral, one of my cousins asked my older brother and me what it had been like to have a father who was an enigma, an aloof presence no one seemed to know. Our cousin had a dad he had turned to and confided in all his life. His question was something I'd never thought about. 'It's curious,' I said, 'but it's the opposite. I never felt a lack. In fact, I always thought he was the perfect dad, quiet, ruggedly handsome, able to make anything. But there was something extra special about him, something we'd consider "primitive" today that, as a child, made me think he was the best dad of them all. I knew, I just knew, that if ever there was any type of problem for me or my family, not only was he there, but he was big enough and strong enough to kick the stuffing out of any other dad in the whole world.' My brother, like our father, not one for many words, listened, smiled, nodded and said, 'That's exactly how I felt too.'

Bruce Fogle is an author and veterinary surgeon.

Anna Ford

Despite everything, I now realise my father was an unhappy man. He was tall and handsome, with an imposing presence, a beautiful voice, but underneath not much self-belief. He hated answering the door or the phone, was basically deeply shy, and yet could be larger than life when holding the floor and telling stories, whilst being the centre of attention. There was anger bubbling away below the surface, all unresolved.

He was isolated as a child and deeply unhappy at his public school, but clung to some of the Edwardian values of his distant parents in thinking that praising children spoilt them. He longed, like many unhappy people, to find that he was adopted and wove (after a few drinks) unlikely tales about his parentage.

I don't remember ever having a conversation with him about anything that mattered. Certainly not about feelings. And we were not allowed to call him 'Dad', it had to be 'Father', 'Papa' or, much later in life, just

'John'. I don't think he meant to be, but he was very class-conscious.

His father wanted him to be an engineer, but being creatively gifted he chose to become an actor. When something turned him against the stage, he married my mother (who he'd met whilst they were both appearing in minor roles in *Romeo and Juliet*), joined the church and settled in the country. But not for long!

His life, and so ours – his five children – became peripatetic. We moved from place to place and school to school, whilst he raged and roared, or sank into a black hole, about the shortcomings of the present parish. But wherever we went he laboured hard to make beautiful gardens.

For him, the grass was always greener, which led us once to emigrate to Canada for three weeks! We returned home to nothing, our furniture still in crates on the boat in Vancouver harbour. But it was a great trip, six weeks across the Atlantic, and up the West Coast of America in an old Dutch cargo boat. The sun shone all the way. Like many Church of England vicars, his belief in God was very individual and I think it ebbed away as he grew older. Many of his parishioners loved him and he must have helped them at difficult times, for he seemed able to do things for them that he couldn't do for himself.

I'm sorry to think he was unhappy and depressed so much of his life, and that these feelings were only temporarily relieved by constantly moving on. His inhibition meant he could never seek help so he took to the grave many unresolved problems.

He also took to the grave his digital watch, which went off in his cardboard bio-degradable coffin as he was lowered into his country grave at exactly 12 noon! It's said people go to stand and listen on the hour to the vicar's watch bleeping from deep below!

Anna Ford is a broadcaster, enjoying a new life out of the public eye.

Sir David Frost

My father was a Methodist Minister and an outstanding pastor to his flock. The most important thing he taught me was enshrined in a Turkish proverb he often quoted, 'Even a stopped clock is right twice a day.' It was all about the intrinsic worth of every human being. Everyone has something to teach you if you are determined enough to find it.

My father did not indulge in potted sermons or dogmatic homilies in daily life. He believed that the best way to capture people's attention or support was by example. He would quote a Sunday School hymn that ran:

The only gospel that some men will read
Is the gospel according to you.

My father did not believe in corporal punishment; a conviction that was unfortunately not shared by all my teachers. In keeping with his generation, my father also did not believe in swearing. Even if he started to use a tame expletive like 'blast', he would catch himself in time to say, 'Blaarn it!' Clearly the word 'darn' had passed the acceptability test!

My father imbued in me his love of books and encouraged me to borrow his encyclopaedia whenever I needed it. I did this for some years until I was writing an essay on Gladstone. The entry in the encyclopaedia concluded, 'He resigned as Prime Minister in 1894 and is now living just outside Cheshire.' It occurred to me that I might not be getting all the benefits of up-to-date scholarship.

He was wise and witty and very happily married. Perhaps that is the most valuable gift a father – or a mother – can bestow: the blessing of a happy home.

Sir David Frost is the only person to have interviewed the last seven US presidents and seven UK prime ministers.

A ROOM
OF MY OWN
Mike Gayle

Once upon a time my office at home was dedicated to me and my individual pursuits: reading, writing, listening to music, and tinkering with my ever-growing collection of eBay purchases. All that's changed. It's now also the spare room when people come to stay, the place where the kids come when they want to explore, and the place where stuff that you don't quite know what to do with comes to rest. While I don't mind its new multi-purpose status too much, at the back of my mind I'm longing for the day when I'll get back a room of my own.

Sitting in my office at home, typing on my computer, I look around the room at all the books, CDs and gadgetry, and I pause for a moment to think about the office my dad had at home when my two brothers and I were kids. Back in the seventies we lived in a three-bedroom council house where space was very much at a premium. My parents were in one room, my two elder brothers in another and then there was me in a bedroom all to myself. So where exactly was Dad's office? In the smallest room in the house, that's where – and no, it wasn't the bathroom. Dad's office was the tiny 'cubby-hole' space under the stairs that most people in our road (the ones that aspired to be middle class, at least) used as a pantry. It was probably only three feet deep and four feet wide and most of that space was unusable because of the slope of the ceiling, but even so my dad still managed to fit in a desk, a stool, two typewriters, all of his back issues of *New Society*, sociology and law text books, while all the time sharing the space with the vacuum cleaner, a tool box and a broken black and white TV. The only natural light in the room came through the frosted glazed window that looked out on to the passageway at the side of the house and, as it had no source of heat, in the middle of winter my dad would have to put on a hat, coat and (for a short while when *The Kids From Fame* were at their peak) legwarmers if he wanted to do any work at all. My dad would be in there for hours at a time, typing away at his dissertation for his MA, or later preparing paperwork for his job at a probation charity, only ever emerging to stretch his legs or make an occasional cup of tea. It can't have been great being cooped up in a room so small he could touch every single wall without even fully extending his arms, and yet in all the time we lived there I never once heard him complain. I'm guessing having grown up in a small town in Jamaica, he was more than a little aware that his own father had probably once dreamed of a room of his own too, and that looking at those four walls in terms of the adage 'it's not where you start or finish that matters, but the distance travelled in between', at the very least the cubby-hole represented a step in the right direction, both for me, my dad and my family as a whole.

Mike Gayle is a freelance journalist and the author of seven bestselling works of fiction.

Ainsley Harriott

As a young boy I remember sitting secretly underneath my dad's Bluthner piano at home, observing his feet pedalling away as he played one song after another. Around him were his showbiz friends, all talking, joking, laughing and drinking Martinis. Occasionally, they would 'jam' and have a singing session together and I would join in by bashing away on the side of the sofa.

My dad was an entertainer for more than 60 years and performed all over the world. Coming from Jamaica, at the age of 17 he won a scholarship to the Royal College of Music to study piano, organ, cello and voice. He became a very successful variety entertainer, able to combine classical, jazz and blues on the piano. I remember going to watch him at the Planet Room in Blackpool's Winter Gardens one summer season. He had the audience in the palm of his hand with his humour, pathos, wonderful energy. He could switch the mood from sentiment to rave-up in an instant.

He loved to cook, and still does. Now that he's retired, he likes nothing better than to entertain people at his home. Even when he's out in the front garden, he talks to the neighbours as if he's still on stage – charming, witty, and thoroughly engaging. Some habits are hard to lose.

I have to admit I have a bit of that in me. It's one of those things, I suppose; we all seem to take on our parents' traits. Sadly, I never learned to play the piano – but hey, Dad can't chop an onion like me!

Ainsley Harriott is a chef, television presenter and the author of several bestselling cookery books.

Joanne Harris

My grandmother always called him Dad. Actually, he was my granddad – Yorkshire born, ex-miner, ex-gardener, always a friend. Never gambled, drank or swore; never borrowed a penny from anyone. Every day, he worked in his garden, wearing rubber boots, a belt made from string, and a faded bobble hat missing its bobble, that had started life off as a tea-cosy. Underneath, he was a magician, an inventor; a some-time poet and a student of life's everyday miracles. He taught me how to make jam and preserves; how to make the most out of a window-box; how to recite the poems of Kipling and Southey; how to recover swarming bees; how to catch tiddlers in a flooded mine-shaft and how to hide a stick in the hedge so you always had one to hand when you needed it. A miner by force of circum-stance, but always a gardener in his secret heart, he started life working down the pit and tending his patch in his spare time; a garden tolerated by his father only because of the food it produced – the flowers hidden beneath cabbage leaves, their cheery faces poking out impudently from between the rows of carrots and runner beans. He dreamed one day of having a garden of his own, with fruit trees and vegetables and flowers by the bucketload. But all his family were coal miners – mining was all they understood.

And then one day, like something in a story – three wishes from a wizened crone who turns out to be a fairy in disguise – someone offered him a job as head gardener in a stately home. The perfect job – a small house of his own; the chance to marry the girl he loved; an orchard, a vegetable patch, acres of flowers and neatly kept lawns…

Then came the war, and he tried to enlist. But years down the mine had made him unfit, and time and again he was refused. And so, he made a sacrifice, quietly and typically without a fuss. He gave up his gardens and his little house and went back home to work down the pit – where he remained for the next 30 years, one of the modest, unsung heroes of that interminable war. And when he retired, lungs blackened by coal dust, he found himself a little allotment, where he went on growing his fruit and vegetables, and worked every day from dawn till dusk, and taught me how to graft a tree, and how to spot wild strawberries under a hedge, and where to pick wild spinach and cress, and how to plant marigolds to banish the slugs, and how to make his blackberry wine, and how to appreciate every minute of sunlight and every waking hour of the day – because, as he used to say, 'You're a long time underground, luv...'

When he died, I emptied his house, and found in his cellar those bottles of homemade wine, labelled Blackberry, 1973, and Elderflower, 1969. I couldn't bear to drink them – there were genies in those bottles, and I wanted them to stay safely inside – although the idea of just throwing them away was equally impossible.

And so I wrote a book about them – a book in which the central character was eerily like my granddad – even down to his tea-cosy hat and string belt – and with the money I bought a house with a garden, an orchard, a vegetable patch...

Most days I can see him there, pottering about

among the rhubarb and spinach, occasionally pausing to pull up a weed or to taste a blackberry on his thumb. It is a kind of magic, of course – but the Yorkshire kind; no fireworks, no fuss.

I like to think that he approves.

Joanne Harris is the author of eight novels, including Chocolat, *which was made into an Oscar-winning film.*

Ben Hewitt

It's the earliest shift of my working life and there's not even a day off. Every morning, by 6.10 a.m., I change three nappies. Three by six-ten. Welcome to my new routine.

I became a dad three years ago and soon we were blessed further with twins. All of a sudden there is barely a moment to catch breath between home-life and work. My wife is amazing and I have every intention of telling her as much – we've booked an evening out next summer.

But alongside a little nostalgia for a previous life, complete with unimaginable luxuries like a lie-in or an evening out, my new routine as a dad has also given me pause for thought. And it's helped me reflect, with gratitude, on my own dad. I was one of four children and, being a dad myself now, I see more clearly what an inspiration the old man has been.

I should tell you a bit about him: he's an activist, a vicar and a musician, a pretty maverick combination. But the overriding character trait in my dad is that he's a man of great conviction, which explains how he has spent his life standing alongside some of the most oppressed communities in the world. And campaigning with them to make a difference in their lives.

Growing up, our home was full of guests and full of surprises – you'd come home from school and never know if you'd be eating with South African anti-apartheid activists, Palestinian peacemakers, Nicaraguan doctors or Dalit liberation theologians! It was like an informal after-school club in international relations – but more fun.

As a singer, making a living by his songs, Dad was often on the road, but 30 years of travel to some of the poorest places on the planet hasn't left him cynical. He finds inspiration in the stories of his friends' daily struggles and always guards against frustration or despair. He has a deep faith rooted in the promise of liberation for those who are struggling – and it's a faith that informs the way he approaches every issue.

Dad always encouraged me to fix my sights beyond the immediate and to look at the bigger picture. And it's no different today – he's always suggesting another way to look at a situation, a way that's rooted in a sense of possibilty and hope. And if that helped me see a situation more positively when I was growing up, it helps me now that I'm a dad too.

It's not all bad, the three by six-ten routine. It gives you a moment to reflect. And as I reflect, I know I want to pass on to my own children their grandpa's spirit of hope, the conviction that change for the better is possible, whatever the challenges we face.

Ben Hewitt is Head of Media for Save the Children.

Charlie Higson

The best piece of advice my father ever gave to me was when he said, 'No writer ever makes any money, so get a proper job and you can always write in your spare time.' I was a teenager when he told me this, and therefore I completely ignored everything he ever said to me. So, thanks to him, I have never had anything remotely resembling a proper job and have had a very happy life doing things I love. My father grew up in the very conservative, convention-bound, pre-war years. He started his working life as an accountant and ended up as a management consultant. I grew up in the sixties and seventies and my favourite TV programme, *Monty Python*, mocked bowler-hatted commuters like him almost weekly. He hasn't worn a bowler hat in years, and is more than pleased that my life took the turns that it did, but it wasn't an iconoclastic TV comedy that changed him, it was the early death of my mother when I was 18. All the expectations he must have had about how his life was going to be were turned upside-down. I think he questioned a lot of his values and beliefs, and realised what was really important. When all this was going on we spent a lot of time together and I got to know him as a real person, not just a 'dad', or a man in a bowler hat. Having boys of my own, I now realise that we can never really know what's best for our children, or have any idea what sort of a world they are going to grow up in. I don't know how my boys' lives will turn out; I just hope that they get to know me as well as I have got to know my own father, and that they ignore any advice I ever give to them.

Charlie Higson is a writer, actor and comedian, and the author of the Young Bond books, as well as four novels aimed at adults.

Les Hinton

Before becoming a father, people say your children will look to you for approval, want you to be proud of them, fear disappointing you, and see none of your faults. When you discover this for yourself, with your first-born, it is a shock.

As they grow, you feel found out. It comes with the first unclouded gaze that sees right through you. Stripped of camouflage, fatherhood suddenly becomes hard.

You do your best to fulfil the duty of shaping them.

But how to strike the balance between too tough and too soft?

How to cure the compulsion to have them inherit your own thwarted ambitions?

How to reconcile to the truth that they can learn little from your mistakes, and must stumble through their own?

You try to teach them simple things: walk towards your fears; never steal another's dignity; never be discouraged by others' estimation of you. One day, of course, they unearth the truth of how often you fail yourself in these things.

Buried as they are beneath the layers of life and difficulty, you worry that your love and pride in them might not be showing through.

You know how often you recognised too late the fragility of their feelings, caused hurt you could never take back, and neglect through your own self-absorption.

They do not always suffer in silence, and nothing quite matches the full throttle of an adolescent's feelings.

You must bear the wounds of their youthful frankness, sometimes grasping the bitterness of Lear, as he cried, 'How sharper than a serpent's tooth it is /To have a thankless child!'

By the time they are adults, all that matters is their health, their happiness, and their friendship. By now the table is turned: you want their approval, want them to be proud of you, fear disappointing them.

And you know that a dad is not altogether a bad thing to be.

You have undying memories: the first touch of a newborn's skin; those early toothless smiles; the faltering three-step staggers; the first hint of those glorious stubborn streaks; the irresistible seduction of a daughter when she wants something; the muddy joy of tiny footballers after a decent game; how they try still to hide their delight in that wonderful not-quite-straight-faced way, when told how good or clever or pretty they are.

As for being a kid, I know how they must have felt now and then – a dad! Who'd 'ave one.

At least, there is the comfort that they were lucky with their mother.

Les Hinton is Chief Executive Officer of Dow Jones & Co, publisher of the Wall Street Journal, *and the father of five – four sons and a daughter, aged from 18 to 37.*

Sir Tom Hunter

Dad taught me about hard graft. The closure of the coalmines took their toll on his grocery business in New Cumnock, and he was forced to shut it down, but he went on to sell at the markets – which is where I spotted the sports shoe opportunity, through analysing his accounts during weekends away from university. You never gave up under my father and you always spotted the opportunities.

He also ingrained in me the need to look after those less well off, something that has led me, over time, to take philanthropy seriously. He led me there.

Campbell Hunter, a proud man of 80 now, still works in our business every morning, five days a week. He keeps all of us on the straight and narrow and sits in on some of our biggest meetings, always chipping in with a thought we'd never considered, but straight on the money.

I don't know there's much more I can tell you about my dad, other than that I hope I can emulate his success with my own kids; the challenge of bringing them up scares me to death. The other thing is, I love him; he's my inspiration and my friend.

Sir Tom Hunter is a businessman and philanthropist, and Founder of the Hunter Foundation which supports educational and entrepreneurial projects in Scotland.

Sir David Jason

I can never remember my father being particularly close or tactile when I was a young boy, and so perhaps that is why I have fond memories of him when I recall a regular outing we used to make.

Each week, my mother and father would take me down the road in Finchley where I used to live, to their friend's house to play cards. I used to take a comic or colouring books or whatever little toy I enjoyed, to while away the time whilst they played into the evening. I remember murmurings of their games, the shuffling of the cards and perhaps the odd chink of coins as they enjoyed an hour or two with their local friends. However, as the evening progressed, I drifted into a weary cosiness and usually ended up dozing off in front of the fire. Now, after all these years, I can feel the strength of my father's arms as he carried me out into the night air, wrapped in either my mother's cardigan or his jacket, and down the road to the comfort of my bed.

I remember the contact of his wool coat and his steady walk, and I'm sure I can remember a snowflake or two drifting on to my semi-conscious little body. I must have been around five or six for my father to carry me so easily, but I recollect that his physical hold was very different to my mother's. Hers was so much more feminine and voluptuous, but I will always remember the strong, supportive arms of my dad.

Sir David Jason is an actor.

MY FATHER IS A TEXTILE AGENT
Lisa Jewell

My father is a textile agent. But to say that my father is a textile agent is a little like saying that the Queen is the Head of State.

My father is a captain in the Territorial Army. He attends all sorts of remarkable ceremonies and banquets and has a wonderful collection of uniforms and medals.

He has an Equity card and is a male model. His face has advertised beer, newspapers and mortgages. When he is 50, he is an extra in the film *Scandal* and can be seen, fully naked, just behind Mandy Rice Davis's beehive.

He collects stamps and first-day covers and commemorative coins.

And he knows an awful lot about birds.

My father loves old cars. At one point, when my sisters and I are small, we have six: a Bentley, an Alvis, two VW camper vans, a Mini and a Ford Escort Mk II in battleship grey. These are mostly out of commission, due to reasons of age and neglect and my father spends an inordinate amount of time in a garage owned by a man called Bert Strawn, trying to ascertain when exactly they will be ready. Bert Strawn I believe, until this day, still has the Bentley. And he might even be dead.

My father plays rugby, every week. Sometimes he takes me and my sisters to the rugger club at Barnet where we tip-toe through the wet, muddy puddles of the communal bathroom. Huge, hairy, naked men surround us singing loud, aggressive songs that echo around the room, and although we are innocent and unversed in the ways of the world, we know that we *do not belong in here*.

My father enjoys gardening and grows tomatoes in our greenhouse.

A former fiancée is from Barbados and my father retains a deep affinity with the island. He owns a pink and mint green chattel house on the beach there and likes listening to calypso music and reggae.

But his favourite music is Gilbert and Sullivan.

He likes antiques. And junk. He picks things off skips

and gets them restored by elderly men in musty sheds in East Anglia. The paving stones outside our childhood home were taken from the side of the road when they were re-paving Regent Street.

My father's friends are numerous and widespread. When we are in town with him, walking through the West End where he has his office, our journey is punctuated constantly by people saying, 'Hi, Tony!' I truly believe he is famous. Every week, when *This is Your Life* comes on the television, I hold my breath, thinking that tonight, *tonight* it might be Daddy's turn.

My father is a sun-worshipper. He sunbathes wherever and whenever he can, with as few clothes on as possible, preferably naked. He squeezes lemon juice into his hands and rubs it into his hair, letting the sun enhance his natural blondness.

My father is a monarchist. He goes to the Trooping the Colour, to the Queen's Parade, to public celebrations of royal birthdays and anniversaries.

He loves London. Every corner of it holds a dear memory for him. He never tires of it and embraces it, warts and all, with every fibre of his being. 'See that room, up there?' he says, pointing to a grimy window in

Soho when I am 16 years old, 'that's where I lost my virginity.' I do not ask to whom, or how old he was at the time, because I am 16 and he has already shared too much information with me. But I am glad that it happened here, in Soho. Anything else would be, well, disappointingly bland.

My father is now 70 but age has not robbed him of an ounce of vitality. He is still a vibrant, eclectic, energetic, life-loving, whirlwind of a man.

And, despite nearly a decade of retirement talk, he is still a textile agent.

Lisa Jewell is a bestselling novelist, whose books include Ralph's Party, Vince and Joy *and* 31 Dream Street.

Dylan Jones

I've always had this sneaking suspicion that Ian McShane's Lovejoy was based on my father, Michael. Admittedly he didn't turn to an imaginary camera every ten minutes and explain just what it was about Lady Jane Felsham that he found quite so beguiling (at least I don't think he did), and he may not have worn a mullet (not successfully anyway), but he was certainly a roguish fortysomething antique dealer who lived and worked in East Anglia. And I was his Eric. Between the ages of ten and 12, I spent every weekend in and out of auction houses helping my father buy old copper kettles, wardrobes, entire dinner services, seventeenth-century landscapes and twentieth-century tat. In market towns such as Swaffham, Brandon, Watton and Diss (basically the Lovejoy backlot), we would scour the auctions and market stalls for all manner of bits and pieces, and things that would often fall apart as soon as we got them home. Having spent a lifetime in the Air

Force, Dad decided that being an antique dealer would be an exciting, and quite possibly financially rewarding, way to end his career. However – and this is one of the many reasons why I'm fairly sure Lovejoy was based on him – the results rarely exceeded expectations, and often fell somewhat short of these. The denouement to my father's career as an East Anglian auction house bohemian came one Christmas Eve, when, having made precisely two and six (about 15p in today's money) from that day's market stall, he decided to climb back into the cockpit and rejoin the RAF. But the reason I remember that time so much is because we not only bonded tremendously well – there was me and him and a whole bunch of tat – but also because it was something I saw him really enjoy. I never knew much about what he did at work – he didn't tell me and I didn't ask – and although he painted, and devoured books, these were fairly solitary pastimes. When we went antique hunting, I could see a passion in him that I hadn't really seen before. And although I haven't really thought it before, not until writing this actually, it probably made me want to pursue a career in something I enjoyed, rather than something that was going to make me a lot of money. I certainly had no intention of joining the RAF.

Dylan Jones is a journalist, author and the editor of GQ *magazine.*

MY DAD
Lorraine Kelly

One of my most vivid memories of my dad is watching Neil Armstrong step on to the surface of the moon, on TV on 20 July 1969.

It is hard now to imagine just how astonishing it was to watch those grainy images.

In the weeks building up to the big event, my dad and I made models of the spindly lunar module that would make the actual landing, as well as the spacecraft that would bring them home.

We drew loads of diagrams, cut out articles from the newspapers, and talked about it all the time. It must have driven my mum mad.

I was ten years old and enthralled by everything to do with astronomy. My dad bought me my first telescope when I was five and, as an extra-special treat I was some-times allowed to stay up really late to watch Patrick Moore in *The Sky At Night*.

No one knew if Neil Armstrong and Buzz Aldrin would actually make it, whether they would land on solid ground, or whether the Russians had in fact beaten the Americans in the space race and were already chilling on the moon.

The suspense when the small 'bean can' that was Apollo 11 disappeared on the dark side of the moon and we lost contact was almost unbearable.

It was history in the making and because my dad fixed TVs for a living we had one of the top-range tellies on which to watch it all unfold.

It was also my dad who introduced me to sci-fi. We used to love watching the original *Star Trek* series and I would sit there saucer-eyed while Kirk and Spock battled with aliens.

I remember queuing up to see *2001: A Space Odyssey* a year before the moon landing, and although I didn't understand all of it (and still don't to be honest), it was an extraordinary film that continues to hold up well today. We talked about that movie for hours.

I asked endless questions which my dad always responded to with great patience.

My dad bought the soundtrack to the movie and a

'stereogram' with new-fangled headphones so we got the amazing 'stereophonic' sound.

My dad also introduced me to the works of Carl Sagan, a true genius who should be required reading in schools across the land.

My dad encouraged both my brother and myself to never stop asking questions and to always be open to new ideas and possibilities. I don't think he could have given me a better start in life, and it definitely helped me both as a journalist and TV presenter.

We remain ever-hopeful of a man landing on Mars and we both still enjoy watching repeats of the original *Star Trek* as well as DVDs of *2001: A Space Odyssey*, *Blade Runner* and *Close Encounters of the Third Kind*, over and over again.

Lorraine Kelly is a journalist and presenter for GMTV.

DAD
Kathy Lette

My dad is called Mervyn. He's an engineer in optic fibre. We call him Optic Merv. In his twenties he was an Australian rugby league player for the Sydney Bulldogs. In fact, for a time, he was famous as the fastest front row forward in the game. All he wanted was four boys whom he could train to tackle and scrum and run... What he got instead were four feisty daughters. The poor man retreated into his garage. And who could blame him?

I suspect all teenage daughters take their dads for granted. He was the nocturnal creature who vanished in the early morning and only reappeared at night. Habits included putting out the garbage, untangling the pool sweep and occasionally locking himself in the guinea pig cage. He was also the recipient of all those strange envelopes with cellophane windows...

To four self-indulgent teenage girls, Dad was just the

tall, muscular figure who could hotwire the car when we'd lost the keys at the beach, save us from cockroaches/mice/floods/bushfires, and catch the pet snake which had escaped *yet again* from my sister's bedroom and was lurking somewhere in the living room. Dad was the one to go out to get medicine from the all-night pharmacist 20 miles away, at three in the morning in the pouring rain. He was the one who took all the film footage of the family – but was never in any of it; just his voice-over, telling us how many miles we'd got to the gallon that day and the exact exchange rate compared to yesterday, or the gradient of the nearest railway line.

He was always our hero, though – the head which was furthest out in the sea, bobbing through the breakers before surfing to shore like a human hydrofoil. He was also the one we sent downstairs to hit the cat burglar over the head with the breadboard. What's more, he could find the square root of the hypotenuse. (Hell, I didn't even know it was lost!) He knows that protons have mass. I didn't even know they were Catholic.

Although not demonstrative (dads of this vintage are emotional bonsai – you have to whack on the fertiliser to get any feelings out of them), he has always shown his love through actions. Every time we girls go home, our fan belts are tightened, tyres pumped, pressure gauges checked, oil changed, and there are suddenly new contact points in the distributor and fresh oil in the differential. (Whatever the devil that is. It's all Swahili to me.) And when he asks me how many miles I'm getting to the gallon – it's the equivalent of a Shakespearean love sonnet.

And even now that we are all married with families of our own, whenever a fuse needs changing or a digital stereo needs mending, or a tax return needs filing or the car needs turning, our mental A to Z is open, the streets mapped and marked – with all roads leading to dad.

I'm pleased to say that Merv now has five grandsons who are all good at sport and at least three of them are showing a healthy interest in the tool-box. Although my dad is too practical and down to earth to ever wear them, it's obviously a case of Designer Genes.

Kathy Lette is a bestselling novelist. Her books including Mad Cows, Girls' Night Out *and* How to Kill Your Husband *are published in 15 languages in over 100 countries.*

Gary Lineker

For me, the greatest thing about being a dad is that your children keep you grounded. My eldest son, George, is particularly good at this. A couple of years ago we were having breakfast and he was reading the newspaper. As always, there was a picture of David Beckham in it. George looked at me and said, 'Wouldn't it be great to have Beckham as your dad?' I asked, 'Why would that be?' and George said, 'Because he's so good at football!' Ha! Ha! Put in my place once again.

Gary Lineker is a sports presenter and former England international footballer.

Joanna Lumley

My father taught us how to ride when I was eight. First we had to know how to groom a pony, how to clean its feet, how to put a bridle together and how to put the saddle on, with three fingers under the girth to make sure it wasn't too tight. We learned to ride with our arms crossed, steering with our knees. We mastered bareback jumping with reins knotted, arms folded, and how to go round the world sitting first sideways on the pony's back, then facing its tail. We were taught that riding is balance not grip, and always to slow down and walk the last mile home. We had to make sure the ponies were properly fed and watered before we could go in for tea. 'Men and horses first,' said my

father; and although I didn't become a
soldier when I grew up I've always kept
that precept close to my heart.
My kind father! How I loved him.

Joanna Lumley is an actress.

Richard McCann

Being a father was something that I had always wanted but never thought I would ever achieve. My own childhood is not something which I can look back on with fond memories. Losing my mother in tragic circumstances at the age of five meant that my siblings and I were eventually placed with our estranged father after spending some months in the local children's home. My father was a big drinker and he became a different person once he was drunk, especially with whiskey, often drunk straight from the bottle. I experienced physical abuse at times, and I feared for years that I had inherited Dad's violence and that it was lying dormant, ready to unleash itself once I had my own family.

Incredibly, in 2006 I became the proud father to Skye, her name taken from the place my mother lived as a teenager, and where Helen and I decided to marry a few months before she arrived. Fatherhood has changed me. I feel as though everything has fallen into place, and something which felt so out of reach for so long is now a reality. The love I have for my daughter is like nothing I have ever experienced. I am the proudest of fathers, and I have surprised myself at just how involved I have been. I have not shirked from my duties either, and I carry out my fair share of responsibilities. One of my proudest moments, as a father so far, occurred a few weeks ago as my wife and I were on our way up the M1 back to our home in Leeds, when we decided to stop at a service station for a refreshment break and to change Skye's nappy. As I am a dab hand at this now, I suggested that I took Skye to the changing station situated in the disabled toilet. I was mid-change when I heard a knock at the door which initially I ignored. The knocking grew louder as I was carrying out, what was to me, routine.

'I won't be a minute,' I shouted, after which the angry woman replied, 'Do you mind? I'm waiting to change my baby here,' possibly assuming I was a bloke using the toilet for myself.

I quickly finished what I was doing and opened the door, with Skye peeping over my right shoulder and the changing bag over my left. I wish I had taken a camera with me as the woman clutching her child won the award for the most embarrassed look of the year. How does the saying go? Never assume… I proudly made my way back to my table with a cracking story to share with my wife.

My wife had our second child, a son, on Sunday 4 November. As with our daughter, his name evokes memories of my mother and family – he is called Ellis, after Ellishadder on the Isle of Skye.

The fear that I was going to replicate my father's behaviour is a thing of the past. I only wish that he could have experienced the joy that fatherhood has brought me.

Richard McCann an inspirational speaker, and the author of Just a Boy *and* The Boy Grows Up.

Richard McNeil

Nothing prepares you for the day you become a dad. Nothing even comes close. Looking back I see a young girl in growing discomfort, carrying a baby in no hurry to be born. The midwife she had grown to trust would not now be there for the birth and had brought along her replacement. The look on my wife's face said it all, but a holiday was booked and there was nothing that could be done.

Our rented house was squeezed into a tired old terrace overlooking the Tyne. The landlord, employed somewhere within Durham University, kept half of the rooms locked up tight. Peeping through keyholes we discovered stolen toilet rolls, tinned foods and unopened cartons of cleaning materials stacked to the ceiling on every available inch of floor. The sheer scale of the larceny had set us giggling like naughty schoolchildren. In our rooms I remember sparse furniture upholstered in dark brown, fading carpets and worn linoleum. My wife had the place shining, everything spotless in readiness, and now in the upstairs bedroom, windows open and curtains closed, she was finding the growing heat of a beautiful morning in early July more and more unbearable.

As promised, the new midwife arrived early to check on things. With her boyfriend waiting in the car she did not stay long. Soon after this, things began to change. My wife grew increasingly fidgety. She tried lying propped up in bed, before sitting in some discomfort on a chair. Finally, trying to gather strength for a trip to the lavatory, she leant wearily over a chest of drawers. I must have been out of my mind to let her attempt this. It meant descending steep wooden stairs to the living room. There were more steps down to a damp little scullery where fungi grew under the sink. Still more, this time concrete, to a backyard at the far side of which lay her destination.

In the cool of the yard I fretted at how long she was taking, unaware that behind the closed wooden door the waters had broken. Somehow we got back to the bedroom. In the hall I dialled the numbers jotted down for emergencies. No answer as I dialled twice, then a calm female voice answered my rising panic at the third attempt. Yes, it was our first baby. Yes, the midwife had been that morning and was due back at four. Time the contractions, and if they shortened I was to let her know. Half the stairs were climbed before I turned. This time I gave her no chance to speak. My wife was alone and in desperate need of help, her baby was about to be born and if things went wrong, she would be responsible. I said this and more in a furious outpouring of panic and rage, before slamming down the receiver.

I told my wife the midwife was on her way. But was she – had I even given her the address? Then a car door slammed in the street below. Looking down I saw a stout little figure bustling towards our front door. She launched into me as we climbed the stairs. Never in all her years had anyone spoken to her in such a manner. Never. This better not be a waste of her time because if it... 'Oh, my dear...oh, my poor lamb.'

I was sent to boil water in every pan we possessed, before returning as instructed to administer the gas and air. Our bedroom that had been refuge from the world was now a charnel-house, where a hanging, drawing and quartering was taking place. It was links of pale blue sausage that finally arrived, squashed most cruelly and wreathed in blood. Things had gone wrong, things my wife must not see. I watched the midwife untangle what I took to be the umbilical cord, then there was a sound of a measured slap. My wife held out protective arms at the first spluttered cry and a most marvellous oxygenated pinkness coloured the angry little face.

'Well done,' the midwife said with a smile. 'Now go downstairs and make us a nice cup of tea.' Waiting for the kettle to boil, the knowledge that I had *not* done well cut through my elation. I should have insisted on hospital when the days dragged on. Or persuaded my mother-in-law to stay. I could have sought help from a neighbour who had children of her own. But I had just sat there until it was almost too late.

Sipping tea we watched over them. Still joined in exhausted sleep, my wife and her daughter, who had finally been born. The afterglow of unknowable magic still lingered in the room. The midwife must have felt it, as she waited for her colleague to return. A fleeting, lopsided little grin scrolled across my daughter's face. She gave a sad little sound, half-yelp-half-sigh. A dad would have picked her up to gently pat away the windy pain. But she did not yet have a dad. There was just a lucky young fool, around whose outstretched finger curled a tiny fist that gripped with a tenacity that surprised him.

Richard McNeil, dad and granddad, retired from directing television commercials to become a farmer.

Sean Macaulay

I was lucky. My parents divorced when I was seven, so I had a dad and a stepdad. It was like stereo parenting. My dad was clean-shaven and loved a pint. My stepdad had a beard and made lists.

It wasn't perfect – shock. In fact, things got so bad at one point that I left home at 18 without a single A-level to my name. But like all great parents, they knew simply to wait. And wait. Until, sure enough, 20 or so years later, I finally became a father myself. Kids are great, but they're no picnic. Even going on a picnic is no picnic with little kids. So now, I feel nothing but compassion and gratitude for my parents' hard work and sacrifice.

Two things especially stand out. First was my step-father's unflappable method for dealing with otherwise overwhelming homework assignments. He could really blow a fuse if he caught you – oh, I don't know – smoking, stealing, making stink-bombs, vandalising the local bandstand, coming home with a number two skinhead cut. But he was never fazed by writing projects, however daunting. He'd simply get out a yellow pad and break the project down into bite-sized chunks, then start brainstorming. After that, taking the first step was relatively easy.

As for my dad, he once admitted that all writing, or rather all not-writing, came down to the same thing – fear. His erratic correspondence and practically extinct birthday cards were testament to that. But he was irreproachably courageous in the area of physical pain. In his twenties, a botched tendon operation meant that he had two toes amputated from each foot. It was especially cruel for him. He was a very sporty guy, who'd once had a rugby trial for Scotland. But I never heard him complain about it. Even when arthritis struck, remorselessly assailing his balance further, he never showed a drop of self-pity. Not ever.

Sean Macaulay is a screenwriter and was the LA Film Critic for The Times *from 1999 to 2007.*

IAN 'SPIKE' MACKINTOSH

Sir Cameron Mackintosh

My dad loved to play the trumpet, and as critic and fellow jazz musician Ian Christie once observed of Ian (or 'Spike' as everyone called him), 'Between his third and eighth drink he was bloody marvellous.'

Months later, he was blown up again in the Egyptian desert during Montgomery's rout of Rommel, at the Battle of El Alamein, and was rescued by some passing Bedouins who took him back to Cairo where he lay unconscious for three months. While recuperating, he was summoned to play for King Farouk whose son loved jazz. Throughout all his adventures, Dad's trusted trumpet never left his side or his hospital bed.

Jazz was his life and he played with a veritable Who's Who of British jazz (Humphrey Lyttelton, Wally Fawkes, George Melly, Sandy Brown, to name but a few). He even played with his hero Louis Armstrong whose style he closely mirrored and, at one impromptu gig, Louis borrowed Dad's treasured Selmar trumpet so that he could join in. However, Dad had to make a living as a timber merchant to feed and educate three hungry boys – especially me – as jazz simply didn't pay that much. The fact that Dad couldn't make music his sole profession had one silver lining for myself and my two brothers, Nicky and Robert, as he always encouraged us to do anything we wanted as a career. His other great example was that he always went through life thinking the best of people – 'jolly good chap' – and was genuinely disappointed if they turned out to be 'a rotter'. This was counterbalanced by our mother's far more beady approach to life.

Having met my mother Diana in Naples towards the end of the war, when they were both working for E.N.S.A., the Army's entertainment division, he was no stranger to the flamboyance of show business, so I had no opposition to my dreams of being a theatre producer, nor did my youngest brother, Nicky, in becoming a chef or my middle brother, Robert, in going into the music business, as both a writer and record producer. Dad still managed to play regularly throughout his life and made several terrific recordings with his colleagues.

In retrospect, one of his other great gifts to us was taking us to see many of the jazz greats in their prime and sometimes introducing us to them after the show. Who could forget the dazzling concerts of Duke Ellington, Count Basie and Louis Armstrong? The brilliant trombone playing of Jack Teagarden, the haunting saxophone of Johnny Hodges, the dazzling piano playing of Art Tatum and Earl Hines, and the unique opportunity of going to an intimate Ronnie Scott's to see Ella Fitzgerald.

Every time I hear these great artists on the radio I go, 'Thanks Dad,' and hear him 'Zaba Doo Zatz' in his inimitable musical 'Satchmo' growl, as he gratefully sips another pint.

Sir Cameron Mackintosh is a theatre producer and impresario.

Dame Mary Marsh

Throughout my life my father, George Donald Falconer, has been a great source of inspiration to me. He studied Classics, qualified in medicine, was a surgeon with the Field Ambulance in the Second World War and returned to work for the rest of his career as a much-loved and respected GP. He was wise and challenging but he also had a great sense of fun.

Games of every sort filled much of our family time together. This was all the more precious given its rarity in his busy life as a doctor working from a surgery based in rooms in our family home. It could range from ball games, including cricket, to I spy in the car, crosswords, Scrabble and card games, which showed his lively competitive spirit most. Doing jigsaws in the caravan on wet days in holidays in the west of Scotland were turned into team races. Of course we were never allowed to see the picture – that was regarded as cheating.

He was a great inventor and, amongst other things, built his own racing car board game based on

Donnington Park, a game we were still playing long after the track itself had shut down. He was also a good and creative storyteller and the tales of ittle bear still live with me, as well as the memory of us all topped and tailed into my parents' bed on a Sunday morning listening to them.

My passion for walking, especially in mountains, comes from my father. In particular, I know most of the fells of the southern Lake District from almost every direction.

I learnt to drive taking him around his home visits to patients in Wallasey. It was a great privilege on those days to have uninterrupted conversations with him, too. I am sure he instilled in me the value of making a commitment in life to seeking to serve the needs of vulnerable people and the wider community, which I have sought to do through my work in education and at NSPCC.

He taught me a great deal about being a good parent and, needless to say, he was a much-loved grandfather, too.

Dame Mary Marsh is Chief Executive of the NSPCC (National Society for the Prevention of Cruelty to Children).

Bill Martin

I was born in Govan, Glasgow, opposite the Govan Fairfield Shipyard in 1938. Two men played an important part in my life – my father, and the now Prime Minister Gordon Brown's father, John Brown.

My father was a great piano player and Gordon Brown's father was the minister at our church, St Mary's, Govan. My parents were married there long before Gordon's father came to the parish.

My old tenement and street are still there, Taransay Street. My father would play the piano at Mr Hamilton the coalman's flat on a Saturday night. Occasionally Gordon's father would turn up there and he would also call on my family during the week – just as he visited everyone during the war, in Govan.

My father obviously gave me my love for music, but the Prime Minister's father said some profound words to me over the years before he left the parish. He told me to join the Lifeboys followed by the Boys' Brigade, and go to church and believe in God, and when I was grown up, to make up my own mind about religion.

Most of all, as I was growing up he told me to follow my heart and my dreams. I did, and a wee boy from the tenements of Govan became the number one songwriter I wanted to be, with the songs 'Puppet on a String', 'Congratulations', as well as many more number ones and top ten hits, and a clutch of show business awards, including songwriter of the year in 1975.

Bill Martin is a songwriter, music publisher and impresario.

David Miliband MP

I remember my dad saying to me that fatherhood utterly changed his life and his perspectives. Cliché but, as I now know, true. He wasn't really the sporty type but my memory of him behind the goal on a rainy Leeds Saturday morning, head in hands, as I, a ten year old trying to emulate David Harvey (Leeds' goalie at the time), let the ball through my legs from a soft shot, is one that will never leave me. It reminds me that fatherhood takes people to new places literally and emotionally; that what at the time seems like a disaster/the end of the world may not quite be that important; and that it is sometimes the small things that matter a lot. I never knew my dad's dad, and my sadness today is that my father is not here to see my children, and they will never meet him. An extra reason for me to pass on those memories – not just about football.

David Miliband MP is Foreign Secretary and Member of Parliament for South Shields.

BOB MILLAR
Fiona Millar

I think about my dad nearly every day. It took me a long time simply to get over the shock of hearing from Alastair, my partner, that he had died. We were at a wedding, in the days before mobiles, and Alastair was paged to leave the marquee to take a phone call. As soon as he walked back in I knew something terrible had happened.

He was definitely a best friend to both of us and also our children's favourite carer. He died eight weeks after our youngest, and only, daughter was born, so that was a double blow.

I miss the fact that he hasn't seen them grow up into exceptional young people and also that I can't ask his advice, which means I frequently think to myself, 'Now what would Bob have done in this situation?'

He could be passionate and stubborn; we didn't speak to each other for six weeks during the 1987 general election period after a ferocious row about the Labour Party's defence policy.

Yet he was also patient, always argued without raising his voice, and used reason and logic to make his point and find compromise where possible. I don't remember him ever smacking me as a child, and during my recalcitrant teenage years he never wavered from combining love with rational argument to keep me on the straight and narrow, for which I am grateful as it eventually led to me passing a few exams and getting to university.

I know I have inherited his political convictions and even though I will probably never completely master his calm, unruffled exterior in the face of a wilful, argumentative child, it will always be an aspiration to be as good a parent as he was.

Fiona Millar is a journalist and campaigner for state education.

Anthony Minghella

I'm sitting on a plane crossing the Atlantic thinking about my father, Edward Minghella. Somebody has just offered me an ice cream from the trolley, I see our family name on the lid of the tub, and there's my dad, immediately summoned. It is easy to imagine him coming to sit here beside me, expansive on the topic of a latest flavour (this one was sticky toffee), projecting his indomitable enthusiasm, his delight in the strength of his grip (worked up from a lifetime of squeezing frozen white dollops into cones), his appetite for a pun, or the capacity for happiness that age has rewarded him with, in place of the ragged tiredness I remember from my childhood.

In reality, I can't recall flying anywhere with my father. Or having travelled with him much at all, beyond the thrilling mile-long march from where the Isle of Wight ferry docks in Portsmouth to Fratton Park to watch football together. That's the indelible journey, struggling to keep up behind a small square man with a determined stride, his hands in characteristic pose, hanging open behind him, impatient to be in the stand, impatient for the match to begin, but also impatient to leave. Sometimes now, when I see film of myself walking away, I see him, am even fooled into believing it is him, the same shining skull thrust forward, the same thick hands.

My father has always been a foreigner. Notwithstanding his 70 or so years in Britain, he has retained the clotted accent of Italy, and the firm perspective of the observer. He's spent his adult life recovering from the poverty of his youth in Frosinone, from the absence of an education, bemused by and impatient of those born into the comforts of his beloved England, with what he views as the failure of so many to grasp the myriad opportunities freely available to them when there was so little opportunity available to him. And in that sense, he is best understood as an immigrant, and for his five children the strongest instruction was always the imperative to grasp these opportunities, to prosper in ways that he and our mother had been denied. They settled, through the most circuitous route, on the Isle of Wight and that distinctive location has worked its specific influence, too, adding another mediation, a strip of water to keep us separate, never truly assimilated. England is not where we are, English not what we are, exactly, but to be glimpsed, *over there* on the mainland.

It seems to me that very little we know or believe or claim about our parents is true. Our sense of their infallibility, or the opposite, the blame we attach to them, the parts they have played in events in which we give them lines or actions, are often unreliable, hostage to the muddle of memory. They invent us, literally, and then we return the compliment, metaphorically. Or perhaps, more accurately, these recollections do not need to be true to matter. In the case of my own family, overstocked as it is with writers, our sibling memories seem to have plundered each other's, so that we are perfectly capable of claiming experiences that are hotly contested by a brother or sister as having belonged, indelibly, to them. I apologise to them all, in advance, for whatever I've stolen in what follows. And our view of parents is so distorted by childhood and its volatility; we are never peers of our parents, but live in that flux of dependency, independence and then their dependency on us. We grow up in front of them; they grow old in front of us.

And the force of them, the imprimatur that settles on our inner beings in the same way it so evidently shapes our looks and physiology, continues to fascinate us but also to elude us; we feel we are wrestling with nurture, moving away from its codes and values, just as surely as we seem to be arriving at them again. Oliver Sachs wrote movingly of an Alzheimer victim with a cruelly brief retention of experience, seconds only, trapped in *hellos*, in the constantly new. He describes the patient meeting a new therapist in his office one morning. He greeted her by offering his hand to shake. In his palm was a drawing pin, which gave the patient a sharp prick. After a normal physical reaction, snatching her hand away, the patient immediately forgot what happened. A month later, she returned to the therapist, oblivious to having been to the office before. Reintroduced, she approached the therapist, her hand open in greeting, only to snatch it away as he offered his. No memory of why, but the knowledge, below memory, of something painful. This tack in the hand seems very profound to me in relation to our parents – and, of course, our children – reminding us that we are shaped more profoundly by what we can't recall, than by what we voluntarily summon. Conjuring our past, its good and bad, is already rendered safe because it is controlled by us, characterised by us, even our most traumatic experiences. Proust and his madeleine, the involuntary recall, prompted by a sound or a taste, or sun on our face, is the more potent and mysterious experience, bringing with it unannounced joy or grief, so just now the sight of an ice-cream tub on a plane, 30,000 feet over the Grand Canyon, brings with it my dad, and a rosary of sights, smells and feelings, clustered around my family name on a lid.

I am perhaps nine, peering from a temporary seat in my father's ice-cream van, which is tricked out, inexplicably, but in the fashion of the period, like a rocket ship, all fibreglass fins and thrusters. He is driving down the Military Road, part of his daily round on the west side of the island. I am attracted to a strange sight – a man with very long hair is strumming a guitar on the back of a motorbike that comes towards us...the man is sitting pillion but in the wrong direction so that as it goes by he is smiling at me as I swivel round to watch him disappear. I shout to my father – 'Look!' and cause him to over-steer, the van swerving from side to side, prompting a gusher of rage that shocks me and that I cannot stem. His fear of an accident, my provoking of it, leaving us terribly bruised for the rest of the journey. Why do I remember that and the first letters of the vehicle's registration: UDL?

Another van, another time, another psychedelic monstrosity, this one brand new, which my father and I are collecting from Crewe and driving back to the island; a rare and delicious treat to be alone with him, to be the special child of five. The van breaks down on a roundabout near Winchester, just dies as it grows dark, and we are forced, to my complete delight, to walk into town and spend the night in a small hotel. We have breakfast together, man and boy, shared emergency experience. Perhaps I remember these moments, simply because we were so rarely alone, any of us with either of our parents. They worked every day of the year in their café, The Mayfayre, opposite Woolworths in Ryde High Street, from the morning until long after we kids were asleep in our bedroom above the kitchen, the noise of which curled up the stairs or crackled through the magic box in our room, a primitive intercom system that would convey clues of each night's kitchen dramas. This is how we knew them – mother and father – in passing, literally, as they hurried from one customer to the next, from the little room we called a factory that adjoined the kitchen – where my father boiled up the ice-cream mix, or scraped it freshly frozen from a gas-cooled stainless steel contraption, exotically complex and Italian, aided by a melancholy man called Dante, and where we kids stabbed little boats of moulds with wooden sticks to make ice lollies – to the kitchen itself, always roasting, always frantic; a world of fridge and furnace.

That café, where the public and private were forever blurred, where our tragedies and successes were played out to a semi-permanent audience of customers and waitresses, is an environment I realise I've recreated for myself as an adult; the world of film-making is remarkably similar. We sit in the cinema and watch intimacies played out, triumphs, tears, laughter, oblivious mostly to how those scenes were made: bedroom scenes observed by a whole crew, by the sound and camera teams; deaths played out with the make-up artist adding a fresh dab of blood, the stunt men in tow. And so I worry now whether I have become, by election, the kind of father my own was forced to be, leaving my children for long periods to make movies; worry that they will complain, in time, that they know me only in passing, as I cook up my own confections around the world, sending love too often by email.

One thing I do know is that I've been blessed to have my amazing father into my own middle-age. I can call him now as I nearly always do – 86, hearty, busy at work, the worst sense of humour in the world – as soon as my plane has landed, and chat for a while about football and ice cream, the metaphors through which we can explain ourselves to each other, just as my conversations with my daughter and son use the language of film, our common ground, for the same purpose. The rest that we dads pass on – the good, the bad, the damage done, the sins of omission and commission, the pride and ambition relayed for better or worse from generation to generation, the tack in the hand – is not ours to know, or calculate. What is true is that my father, moral compass, is still the first person I want to share my best moments with; I hope that Hannah and Max feel the same, but also, sometimes, that I can be the ear for their failures and their disappointments. That is what a dad is for. I remember a mug Hannah gave me when she was a child. It was decorated all over with words defining what a father was supposed to be. I've forgotten them all now, except *Storyteller*, except *Bank*, except *Friend*.

Anthony Minghella was a writer, director and producer. His films have been nominated for 24 Academy Awards and 36 Bafta Awards.

Anthony Minghella sadly passed away as this book went to press.

THE WISH LIST
Andrew Motion

You also took these with you underground:
your check Viyella shirt; your regimental tie;

a too-late letter from your grandson Jesse Mo;
your Book of Common Prayer. On second thoughts

make room for these things too: the china hare
I lifted from your bedside table years ago,

and kept to prove I loved you like a child;
your father's bone-backed hairbrushes

worn down to fuzz; the gilt St Christopher
you carried through the war; your army pack

DADS

for D-Day with its German phrase book and a map
of Normandy; your snaps of Berlin station

with the roof blown off; Mum's wedding ring;
the yellow dress she wore on honeymoon;

your City suit; your bowler hat; your brolly
furled and dusted with dry flecks of rain;

your season ticket for the London train; your pen;
your leaving portrait with the twisting hands;

your hunting breeks; your crop; the Gammage cap
a swallow bull's-eyed in the stable yard; your box

of fishing flies; your rod and net; your waders
hanging in the garage upside down; your pullover

with pockets bulged like fists; your specs;
your blotter scarred with hieroglyphs; your Bensons

and your TV guide; your *Telegraph*;
your diary with its pale blue empty pages;

your appointment card; your vase of floppy roses
Kit brought from the garden; your electric bell;

your stone-cold tea; your straw; your cardboard bowl;
your Kleenex box; your photograph of home;

your radio still cranking out *Today*; your dying word
which, though I held my breath, I never heard.

*Andrew Motion is Poet Laureate and Professor of Creative
Writing at Royal Holloway, University of London.*

Baroness Neuberger

One of the earliest memories I have of my
father is sitting down with him to learn the
words of a Hebrew song, 'Maoz Tsur',
'Rock of Ages', the song we sing at the
festival of lights in the winter, Chanukah.
I couldn't read Hebrew yet – I must have
been three or four – and he sang it through
with me over and over, so patiently, that
I still have the sound of his voice in my mind
when I sing it, and it is 11 years since he
died. I think his incredible patience might
have been because he had been somewhat
embarrassed a few days earlier when I had
sung – as a nice Jewish child who didn't
celebrate Christmas – 'Away in a Manger' at
the top of my voice right outside the Chief

Rabbi's house. I had just learned it at nursery school. No wonder my father was so patient in the teaching, but he was always a patient teacher – and a fantastic father, who gave me total encouragement in everything I wanted to do.

Baroness Neuberger is a social reformer, rabbi and member of the House of Lords.

Tracy-Ann Oberman

My father's watchword was honesty.

He always said that a person's good name was the only thing of worth that they leave behind when they die. It doesn't matter what riches, fame or success they may achieve during their lifetime; it is their honesty and integrity and the way they treat people that will be their imprint on this world. There was something very spiritual about this. He treated waiters and waitresses, cleaners, the *Big Issue* seller outside his office, as if they were crowned monarchs. Anyone who might have been intimidated by his Cambridge degree, or the cut of his suit, were immediately put at ease by a kind word and an ability to make them feel as if they were the most important person on the planet for the duration of their time with him. He would have made a wonderful member of the royal family.

Fiercely intelligent, witty, funny, yet conversely extremely shy, he could light up a room just by being in it. He was my personal hero and the world felt like a much safer and better place by his being in it.

Never one to avoid a family confrontation, I could argue with my mother, sister, cousin, uncle, for hours, but with my father I always wanted to protect him. And he always wanted to protect everyone else he loved too. He was a fixer, always knowing exactly the right thing to say and do at any given moment. It didn't matter how trivial the problem. He would talk long into the night with my sister and me, trying to sort out whatever it was that was bothering us, be it homework assignments, boyfriend troubles or existential angst.

In the early years of my acting career, when things were not moving as swiftly as I would have liked and I wasn't getting the roles I craved, I remember him looking at me and saying, 'Tracy, you are like a William Morris wallpaper. You won't suit every room or building, but when you find the right setting you will transform it and make it something truly wonderful.'

Lawyers are not known for being beloved. Shakespeare said in *Henry IV*, 'First Kill All the Lawyers.' But my dad was totally adored by his clients and the legal profession alike. He was honest and committed to their well-being. We'd often never see him during the week or even at weekends because he was working, poring over contracts for them and soothing their anxieties over the phone. But other than my mother, no one was able to soothe his anxieties. As a young man he lost his father, mother and aunt in the space of a year. His world was rocked and he mistrusted so much of life in case it dealt him another body blow. Work was a solace, it was controllable and it was possible to bury loss in hours and hours of logic and fact. His favourite quotation was 'like flies to wanton boys are we to the gods, they kill us for their sport'. A cynical, absurdist view of life and yet conversely he was deeply spiritual, and deeply creative. After his death we found a notebook of his writings, including five chapters of a novel that he had written. It was very good. He could tell a story like no other, he could charm the birds from the trees with his warmth, he could've schmoozed Stalin with his charm, big blue eyes and dark hair.

Everyone thought they were his intimate, everyone loved and admired him, and yet I realise no one actually knew him, probably not even his daughters. He was way too complex and layered for this world. Passion and creativity hid under a façade of logic, a love of football and sport, a man equally at home with a Latin primer as a copy of the *News of the World*, a natural raconteur, a showman who hated the limelight, a people person who craved privacy, daddy to everyone yet 'daddied' by none, the safety net for everyone he met and yet unsafe in himself.

I miss him so much because he was love and strength and kindness, but also slightly distant.

He died in my arms ten years ago, long before he could have the pleasure of seeing his wayward, troubled, angst-ridden daughter achieve professional and personal success and happiness. He would have loved his granddaughter, born last year, because when I look at her she has his qualities: fierce intelligence, a loving affectionate inclusive nature, a total scene stealer, humour par none, the most beautiful eyes and smile, and yet a need for independence.

Tracy-Ann Oberman is a television, theatre and radio actress, she is also a playwright and writer.

THE 88-YEAR-OLD NEW WRITER
John O'Farrell

At the age of ten my father walked back from school towards his family home. All the other children in the street were waiting for him and followed silently behind to see him go in the house where earlier in the day the curtains had finally been drawn closed. They all knew what this meant. Mrs O'Farrell had finally passed away. Little Gerald had lost his mother. The other kids just wanted to see what happened next. Well, he opened the door and went in. And his life was utterly changed from that moment onwards.

My father never complained about having lost his mother so young; he's always had a positive 'Ah well, not to worry' attitude to life's problems. Perhaps the experience of such an early bereavement or being dive-bombed by Stukas during the retreat from France puts life's little irritations in perspective. Well, that and a couple of pints of Brakspear's Bitter. Some people are 'glass half-full' types, others are 'glass half-empty'. My father has always been 'glass completely empty; let's have another one'. Much of my teenage education occurred in the snug bars of local public houses at the weekend. When most adolescents are barely communicating with their parents, we sat around in pubs putting the world to rights and confidently predicting that Mrs Thatcher would never become Prime Minister. And we laughed a lot. Even today at 88 years old when his senses are failing him, registered blind and unable to find his hearing aid, his sense of humour is still as sharp as ever. I saw him the other night and he complained as my mother prevented him from turning up the gas fire. 'When I'm being cremated she'll still be saying, "You've got the gas up too high."'

My father didn't talk much about his mother during my childhood. But now as a parent of teenage children myself and with him nearing the end of his life, I've started to ask him about what she was like. And I've begun to wonder if my own career as an author was the one my father was denied. When he lost the one person who had nurtured his love of literature and ideas, the writer in the family had to wait. In an ordinary, working-class Irish family, she had been the intellectual who had raised his eyes to a world of books and possibilities. Perhaps if his teenage years had continued to have the encouragement and nurture of his aspirational mother, 'Gerald O'Farrell the author' would have eventually flowered. Instead she had left him with just enough to pass on to me. His father, on the other hand, had just gone to the pub all the time. Obviously I never do that.

My father recalls a poor performance in his interview for the local Catholic grammar school, but they asked him why he was wearing a black armband and the blunt explanation may have caused them to look kindly upon him. Although he failed to prosper academically at the Xaverian College, his English teacher thought him promising enough to secure him a job interview at *Reynolds News*. Of course his mother would have worked hard to prepare him for the interview, bought him copies of the paper to read beforehand and smartened him up for the big day. Instead he made his own way there and arrived unprepared. They started off by asking this shy Irish teenager some questions in French. Or maybe it was Latin. The fact he wasn't sure which was probably not a good sign. Still hoping to be the first O'Farrell to work with his brain and not his hands, he plucked up his courage and walked up to the grand doors of the *Manchester Guardian* to ask them for a job. He was 16 years old, without any qualifications in the middle of the Great Depression. The *Guardian* might have been liberal, but it wasn't *that* liberal. I didn't hear this story of him being briskly ushered out of reception until 60 years later when I rang him to tell him I had been offered my own weekly column in the *Guardian*. He was almost overcome with pride. His son would be writing for the paper he had read all his life, in the pages that he'd dreamed of writing for himself in another life. And for the five years that I wrote the column, he would ring me up every week without fail to tell me that today's column was 'my best yet'. When his eyesight became too poor to read the newsprint, I would post him his own personal copy, in super 'shout-at-the-reader' 24-point print. Then even that became unreadable and so I would record the column on to a cassette each week and post that to him. 'Marvellous, John! Your best yet!' would come the reliable message on my answerphone.

My own interest in writing had been gently nurtured by my father during my teenage years. A booklet entitled 'Writing For the BBC' was subtly left in my bedroom, and copies of humorous books were picked up in second-hand bookshops. 'I'm looking forward to hearing your jokes on the television,' he said to me once when I'd made him laugh, and I blushed that he had guessed my secret ambition. But while my teens were spent penning submissions for the school magazine and idly thinking about doing English at university, he had wandered around 1930s' Manchester looking for work. 'Grim-up-North' unemployment was finally brought to an end by the personal intervention of Adolf Hitler. Dad spent six years in the Royal Signals (Light Ale Division). He was one of the last out of Dunkirk, probably because he spent so long in the duty-free shop. He was eventually posted to India where he listened in to Japanese Morse code signals and passed the messages on to British intelligence. If these were anything like the phone messages he took for my mother, he probably remembered them three days later. 'Oh, I forgot to tell you, darling. The Japanese are invading Burma.'

He wrote poems in India and a couple of them were published after the war. Alongside other 'new writers' such as Frank O'Connor, he appears in a dog-eared hardback collection that I keep in my office. It's called *Modern Reading* and cost two shillings. But then came the pram in the hall and his muse got fed up of waiting for him to commit. 'Caged birds don't sing,' Dad used to say, just to wind up my mum. Somehow his love of books ended up with him lugging huge boxes of them in and out of the boot of his Morris Traveller. Frankly I think he would have been a better writer than he was entrepreneur. He set up his own business as a book dealer, rebinding old hardbacks in leather and exporting them to the United States. When he had a big order on, he would employ one of my brother's friends to help him pack up all the books for export. And at lunchtime they would have a couple of pints and my dad would say, 'You know Steve, I think I should give you a pay rise.'

'No, Mr O'Farrell, you gave me a pay rise after we went to the pub yesterday. I can't have another one.'

'No, no...' he would insist, 'you're working really hard; I think you deserve a rise...' and by the end of the week his embarrassed teenage employee was trying to find ways of leaving his excessive overpayment on my dad's desk.

But in between rebinding the great novels of Charles Dickens and Anthony Trollope, my father was secretively working on a book of his own. I'd take him a cup of tea at his desk, and he would guiltily cover up the handwritten manuscript and return to columns of figures that didn't quite add up. Eventually he finished it, but not knowing his way around the world of publishing or literary agencies, he optimistically sent out his *magnum opus* to be added to the huge pile of unsolicited manuscripts blocking the corridors of various unsuitable publishing houses.

Maybe the unfulfilled literary career would have been no different if his mother had lived; maybe he would have been like the thousands of aspirant authors who attend creative writing courses or send in overlong novels charting one man's battle against a blind and over-cautious publishing industry. Except that I read my dad's book and I thought it was pretty good. And so for his eighty-eighth birthday I got it published. I did attempt to explain to him the process whereby I fed the hand-typed text into a scanner then uploaded the file on to a self-publishing website, designed a cover and then ordered a number of printed copies from Lulu dot-com.

'Lulu the singer?'

'Er, no, listen, don't worry too much about how it's done, Dad. Suffice to say, I've got you a dozen here to send to friends and family and I can get you as many copies as you want.'

'Where are they all – in your loft?'

'No, they're in Lulu's loft. And Sandy Shaw's got the rest of them.'

'Don't be bloody cheeky...'

He hugged the book to his chest with delight and pride; an 88-year-old new writer. Just making out the photo of the old Irish thatched cottage on the cover, he declared that was exactly like his auntie's house back in Galway, where his thinly disguised childhood memoir is set. It was where he was sent to spend the long summer holidays after his mother died. Maybe if she had lived there would have been many more novels, but when those curtains were drawn in 1930, the writer in the family was forced to skip a generation.

'Ah well, not to worry,' he says, when I tentatively

suggest this to him. 'How are you getting on with your history book?'

'It's going well...' I tell him. 'And the advance came through yesterday...'

'Good...' he says, and I think this is because he is proud that his son writes for a living, '... because it's your round. Now, I've been thinking about that idea you had for your next book...'

John O'Farrell is an author, broadcaster and comedy scriptwriter.

MY DAD
Jim O'Neill

My dad was a strange old inspiration to me, but the more my life goes on, the more I realise how important he was. He left school when he was very young, and was denied the chance to get any real education, having to work to contribute to his family's income. I have still never quite figured out how, but he had an amazing interest in being 'informed', and ensuring that my three sisters and I were driven in pursuing our life goals. He would constantly make us all (including our mum) suffer by listening to Radio 4 – especially the six o'clock news – and in the mornings, if we didn't get up for school when we were supposed to, he would play 'A Life on the Ocean Waves', a Royal Marine favourite, on our very basic record-player and not take it off until we were up. Any vague mention of 'How did United get on last night?' would be met with a sharp rebuke (and plenty besides in those less permissive father–children days!), and I guess this instilled a great sense of purpose, duty, courtesy and respect in the four of us. Despite having a modest income as a Post Office employee, he was driven to ensure that we all had the best educational opportunities possible. He could never have afforded it, but insisted I tried to go to the best secondary school in Manchester. (The fact that they didn't play football meant I was very pleased to have flunked the entrance exam!) That drive was with him till he passed away three years ago. Close to the end, one of my sisters apologised for not bringing her son, his grandson, to see him in hospital. His muffled answer, even then, was, 'The best thing he can do for me, is finish his degree and get good grades.'

Jim O'Neill is Chief Economist at Goldman Sachs, responsible for all their economic forecasts and the team around the world.

Alan Parker

Early mornings with my father are vivid
memories. He always turned on his light at
5.30 or 6 a.m., his writing and reading time.
By the time we all tumbled downstairs and
collided in the bathroom, he would be
in his stockinged feet, playfully reciting
Shakespeare or a verse whilst asking
us about the day ahead.

He would come down with a bulging
briefcase but always with a book in it. Ready
to face the day with 'your shoulders back',
and doing what it takes to 'make the most
of whatever lies ahead, good or bad'.

I would play-box with him as he taught us to be 'on the balls of your feet' and 'always balanced'. Always giving advice, 'never watch your opponent's gloves, you always watch his eyes, they tell you everything', and 'if you make them laugh you can keep hitting them on the nose and they never mind'.

A bubbling, embracing life-force, playful and serious as he encouraged us to give it everything, our very best. Anything else would be a waste of the day.

Alan Parker is Founder and Chairman of the Brunswick PR Group.

Charlie Parsons

We tend to think that our generation has come up with the best answers to everything but many of my dad's values make more sense than today's. My dad was born in 1909 and was 'green' long before the term was invented. It wasn't just a wartime mentality of saving string: he simply couldn't bear waste – so much so, he'd do anything to prevent it. Sometimes it could result in strange recipes conjured from the previous day's meals. People nowadays might mistake this for meanness but actually he was, alongside this, the most generous person I've ever known. When a grandfather, no visiting child could come away without a gift, always homemade from something else or something strange like a potato – and always, because of that, much appreciated. Nowadays everyone is to some extent 'green' but the emphasis on using different kinds of energy is different from his driving force of loathing waste.

My dad was a bit of a character. He loved a joke, a

good story and a practical joke. Despite facing some quite rough times – dealing with his brother's death in a sporting accident, often being unemployed in the 1940s, '50s and '60s, trying to make ends meet as he brought up five boys, losing his sight when he got older – he never stopped appreciating life and revelling in it. He also took an extraordinary interest in the world around him, loving people who bucked the system. My dad always recognised and appreciated ideas and people that were out of the ordinary, not caring for homogeneity. He always wanted to deal in a practical way with life. That's why his heroes were men of action like Montgomery or Churchill. But you could never quite predict who he would admire – he loved Mick McManus the wrestler. And despite being a lifelong Conservative supporter, he loved the 'Beast of Bolsover', Dennis Skinner, for being so Bolshy.

I'm a lucky fellow for having been brought up by a man who loved life, but never doubted that ideas and people should be questioned. What an inheritance!

Charlie Parsons is a television producer, whose credits include Survivor, The Big Breakfast *and* The Word.

Lord Patten

My only piece of wisdom about fatherhood is based on my own experience: talk nicely to your dads while you can, because they are not going to be around for ever.

Lord Patten of Barnes is a statesman and politician.

FATHER AND SON
Gervase Phinn

My father was typical of many Yorkshire folk: industrious, plain-speaking, generous and cheerful, with strong views and a wry sense of humour. After coming out of the army (he was a dispatch rider with the Royal Artillery and a member of the Army Equestrian Team) he became a steelworker at the great foundry of Steel, Peach and Tozer. His correct title was 'de-seamer' and he spent his working life chipping out faults in the metal ('scarfing') as the steel billets rolled out in the finishing bank. As the steel emerged it might have a 'seam' or a defect which had to be removed, otherwise when the metal was rolled out there would be a fault. Nowadays, a sophisticated machine using oxygen jets blows the debris away and the de-seamers can remain relatively clean. In my father's day de-seaming was a filthy job of work.

As a boy, on my way to watch Sheffield United (my eldest son Richard is, thank goodness, an avid fan) I remember well the bumpy bus ride from Rotherham to Sheffield via Attercliffe, past the place where Dad worked for 30 or more years. Down the depressing Don Valley rattled the blue and white double-decker bus, past dirty corrugated-iron sheds, yards of scrap, rusty cranes and huge overhead transporters. It was an area that contained little but dust, dirt and an incredible ugliness. Years later, when I visited the magnificent Magna, the industrial museum now sited in the Don Valley, it was only then that I fully realised what an unpleasant and dangerous job my father had had and what a very special man he must have been to have gone into that hell day after day, night after night, and never complain. Most of us want a job that offers some variety and challenge – to go into work in the morning and look forward to something different. But the de-seamer had to go into work day after day with the same predictable, monotonous and intensely dirty job to do. And the fact that my father did that job without moaning or getting moody or angry with us children seems to me to be remarkable.

Near the River Don in Rotherham was the swimming

baths, and most Saturdays Dad took the three boys
down for an hour in the warm, pale green steaming
water, so strong in chlorine that our eyes streamed for
a good half hour after the session. In the entrance was a
large bronze bust of Captain Webb, a national hero who
swam the English Channel in record time. His healthy
moustachioed face used to appear on the front of match-
boxes. It seems odd, of course, in this day and age, that
such an athlete and national hero should be used to
advertise matches which were the smokers' constant
companion. On the way into the changing rooms the
children would rub Captain Webb's nose for good luck
so the only part of the noble effigy that shone brightly
was the aquiline proboscis.

It was not unusual, as we were getting into our trunks
(those terribly itchy woollen affairs with canvas belts and
metal clasps), to see a rat running between the cubicles.

'Watch tha feet!' the attendant would bellow from
the side of the swimming bath. 'Theere's a rodent on
t'premises.' This would be followed by the screams and
yelps of terrified children, frantically scrambling up on to
the wooden seats in the cubicles.

'Geeaw, wi' all that racket, yer daft 'apeths!' the

attendant would shout. 'It's more freetened o' thee, than thy are of it.'

As I cowered on the wooden seat, I wasn't at all convinced. We would then hear scuffling and running as the attendant chased the intruder with a long bamboo pole he used to teach the children to swim. 'Come 'ere yer little bugger!' he would shout. Following our swimming session Dad would take us into the café and we would have mugs of hot sweet tea and teacakes. I used to pick out the currants before eating the soft bread and watch the swimmers emerging from the changing rooms, hair slicked down, red shining faces and giving off the overpowering smell of chlorine.

My father was an incredibly patient man and taught all his sons to swim in record time. It was because we all had such implicit trust in him that we willingly let go of the side of the bath. 'It's all right,' he would say, 'I'm here. I won't let you drown. You'll be fine.' It wasn't long before I was splashing up and down the baths. My brother Alex was the swimmer in our family though and could slice through the water like a knife. Later he swam for the school and won most of the races, much to the delight of our father who never missed a gala.

On one occasion, I must have been about eight at the time, Dad said we were going to the baths with a friend of his and his son. In the car he told me that I would be meeting Reg whose son Francis went to a special school and was about my age. I was warned to be on my very best behaviour and make a bit of an effort with Francis who hadn't many friends. I thought this Francis would be like the boy at the top of the hill who went to Rudston, the posh private school on Broom Lane, that he would be toffee-nosed and full of himself. I had no idea what a special school was. When we arrived at Reg's house, I fully expected to see this boy waiting on the step dressed in a coloured blazer and wearing his fancy cap. I followed Dad into the front room to find Reg's wife sitting on the settee with the boy face down across her lap. She was rubbing some ointment into his bottom. The boy wore nothing but a thin white vest. I didn't know where to look or what to do but stayed rooted to the spot. None of the adults seemed the slightest bit awkward or self-conscious and continued to chat away. The little boy himself didn't appear at all embarrassed and looked up at me and smiled. If Mum had done that with me, I would have prayed that the floor would open and swallow me up. I could see now that the boy was handicapped.

'Nearly done,' said Reg's wife, pulling on some sort of plastic pants. 'Francis has been so looking forward to today. He loves the water.' The boy made a gurgling sound and threw his head back. 'This is Gervase,' she continued, 'and he's come to take you swimming.' My heart sank into my shoes. I was unsure and frightened. At school the word 'spastic' was used as a term of abuse. 'You spastic!' boys would shout if you missed a shot at the goal or did something stupid. I had passed so many times the plaster figure of the smiling boy with callipers on his legs holding the charity box that stood outside Davey's Café in All Saints' Square, but had never met a real spastic. And now I was to go swimming with him. Suppose my friends were at the baths? What would they say? And why hadn't Dad told me?

The wheelchair was put in the boot and we set off for the swimming baths with Reg next to my father in the front of the car and me sitting with Francis in the back. The boy smiled a lot and pulled funny faces, and when he tried to speak he dribbled. I remember feeling so embarrassed at the baths, seeing people staring at us as we headed for the water and I quickly swam on my own into the deep end instead of playing in the shallows with Francis. I made no effort at all to be friendly or kind. When my Dad waved for me to come and join them I flipped beneath the water and ignored him.

Dad didn't say a word as the four of us left the baths. Reg thanked me for coming and Francis smiled and nodded. I felt awful. On the way home I could see that my father was angry with me. He dropped Reg and Francis off and after we turned the corner, he pulled over and switched off the engine.

'I think you should be ashamed of yourself, young man,' he said quietly. He only called me 'young man' when he was mad at me. 'I am very disappointed in you.'

I hung my head and mouthed, 'I'm sorry.'

'I should think you are,' said Dad. 'It costs nothing to be friendly and Francis is just like any other boy but he's got a lot more than most to put up with.'

'I'll play with him next time,' I promised.

'I shouldn't think there will be a next time after the way you behaved today,' said Dad, starting the car. And he never said another word. I can't recall my father getting angry very often but that day I remember well his quiet voice and the look in his eyes and I still feel bad about that day at the swimming baths. I never did get to play with Francis.

I cannot remember my father ever shouting or swearing or smacking me. I just picture a small, quietly spoken, loving man with fingers as fat as sausages, a shiny bald head and a smile which lit up my world.

Gervase Phinn is a former schools inspector for Yorkshire, now a bestselling author.

Libby Purves

When I was between the ages of nine and eleven, my dad was British Consul in Lille, a dourly homely city in the north of France. I was sent to the local convent school, 66 Rue Royale, and learned French at high speed. We were four children, but the two youngest boys were small and my other brother was at boarding school in England, and since Dad got more at ease with his children the older they were (his generation was not generally acclimatised to babycare), I had him to myself quite a bit. Especially in the evenings, if Mum wanted a quiet time in.

So my best memories are of us two setting out on foot to the Rue de Bethune where the cinemas were, to look for the scariest, silliest posters – huge action movies like *The Long Ships*, about Vikings and women in fur bikinis, or clunky dinosaur films, or sometimes moody black-and-white films about love affairs which ended badly.

We would pretend that this was to improve my French, because they were often subtitled and we would crow with glee at the awful translations. But really we were just out on the town, out on the toot, enjoying the flashing neon signs and the adventure of the urban night. On the way back we'd have a sneaky *croque monsieur* from a pavement stall in the Grand' Place. Best nights out I ever had, bar none.

Libby Purves is an author and broadcaster.

THINGS I LEARNED
FROM MY FATHER
David Puttnam

My father could find room for the
word 'fair' in the resolution of *any* problem,
large or small; and he always thought of
'envy' as being an illness.

My father taught us that it was impossible
to please all the people all of the time.

That inevitably there would be those
with whom you would, on occasion,
profoundly disagree.

The important thing was to choose your enemies with as much care as you chose your friends, as eventually *both* would come to define you, and everything you stood for.

After he died I found this quotation pinned to the underside of the lid of his desk:

'Be true to the dreams of your youth.'

He always was.

Lord Puttnam is an award-winning film producer, whose credits include Chariots of Fire, The Killing Fields *and* Local Hero.

FATHERS AND SONS

Ian Rankin

I've been putting off writing this piece because I wasn't sure if I wanted to write about my own father or being a father myself. Yesterday, however, I was attending an event in Edinburgh and a man came up to tell me that his father and mine had been great friends at school. I decided this was a sign – I would sit down this morning and write about my cartographic dad. Before I could start, however, my 15-year-old son came into the room. He'd been listening to some snippets from a Bonzo Dog Band CD I'd just bought. We then got talking about humour in music, and I dug out a few LPs, wanting him to hear various bits and pieces. For most of his life, my son has shown no interest in 'popular' music, but Frank Zappa and the Bonzos seem to have caught his imagination, and at last I've got someone to listen to all those old LPs with.

By the time I was becoming interested in music, both my sisters had left home. I was 12 and would buy all the pop music papers, decorating my room with the free posters culled from each week's copy of *Sounds*. My parents never complained. I was buying music, too. LPs and singles would be played on an old Dansette which had belonged to one of my sisters. But one Christmas my parents saved up to buy me a cassette player. Frankly, this sealed their doom. When we sat of an evening or weekend afternoon, playing whist or Scrabble or dominoes, the machine would provide musical accompaniment – Alice Cooper or Roxy Music, T Rex or the Rolling Stones. Again, my mum and dad never complained, though Mum almost had heebie-jeebies that same Christmas, crossing the threshold of a dark and odorous record shop in Kirkcaldy to buy me a requested Jimi Hendrix album.

My dad and I didn't bond over music. He was 40 years older than me, and seemed to prefer Max Bygraves to Marc Bolan. Instead, he took me to football games, and at home we did the newspaper crossword together. He cracked jokes, told funny stories from his youth, and whistled everywhere he went. He'd left school at 15 and got a job in a local grocer's, eventually running his own branch in Lochgelly. In his fifties, he became unemployed. After a short stint at a supermarket in Cowdenbeath, he applied for a job at Rosyth Dockyard, preparing marine charts for the submarines. I was in my mid-teens by this stage, and had graduated from junior high to senior high. We had fun filling in one of the school forms, deciding to describe his occupation as hydrographic cartographer – so all those crosswords really had served their purpose!

Neither my father nor my mother lived to see me become a successful novelist. Nor were they around to be grandparents to my two sons. That's a hell of a shame, because I know my dad would have loved refashioning all those old stories, and maybe kicking a football around the garden, and telling his grandkids about the war, the grocery trade, and his short but happy career as a hydrographic cartographer.

Ian Rankin is an author and creator of the bestselling Inspector Rebus crime fiction series.

Ruth Rendell

My father was a great reader but he used to assert that he never read books written by women. However, he did read two or three of mine. Out of a sense of duty, I suspect, as he never told me what he thought of them. Hardy was his favourite author and he used to read him aloud to me, an ordeal I endured because I loved him and didn't want to hurt his feelings but it put me off Hardy for a long time, though I came at last to enjoy his work.

Rather endearingly, he was a stranger to alcohol and an innocent. The one and only time he took my mother into a pub he ordered cider and thought the barman would bring him a bill to their table. Whisky was anathema to him. He only drank it twice. The second time was at a drinks party he was badgered into attending as a newcomer to the neighbourhood. How he came to accept a whisky I don't know, but I suspect he was told it was Scotch and thought that was different. It reminded him of a dreadful occasion when 'your uncle

Henry Kruse' bought him a whisky in the Great Eastern Hotel before getting into a train at Liverpool Street station. For some reason, he always referred to his brother-in-law like that, always by his Christian name and surname, as he did everyone he disapproved of, regardless of how well he knew them or how closely connected to him they might be.

Another brother-in-law was Otto Waldorff. Uncle Otto never drank whisky, as far as I know. He had other failings in my father's eyes, among them an inflated idea of his own importance. An injury to one of his legs kept him bed-bound for a few days and my cousin Sonia, a charitable infant – he had never been very nice to her – commented, 'Poor Toto, bad egg.' When it was passed on to him, this remark disproportionately delighted my father. He immediately ceased calling Uncle Otto by his full name and from then onwards he became Poor Toto, or simply a bad egg.

Baroness Rendell is a bestselling mystery and crime fiction writer.

Gary Rhodes

As a father, there are many special moments to be remembered with your children. I have two sons, Samuel, 19, and George, 17.

However, the one that stands out for me takes us back a good few years now. A favourite dish for them both is a tasty chicken and pasta carbonara. It was on one particular occasion that I suggested we each make, the boys and myself, fresh pasta using three different recipes. The recipes were scribbled on paper, folded, and picked. George, the youngest, had first choice. He wasn't too pleased to find his recipe was to be made by hand, no machinery, with no flashy ingredients of egg yolks or olive oil; it was the most basic of the lot. Sam was jumping up and down with pleasure, a food processor with yolks to enrich; and me, the electric mixer with olive oil.

The special moments were about to begin, watching their faces as textures were introduced to one another, shapes, colours and flavours all in motion. After resting and rolling, some by hand, some by pasta machine, we decided to hang the tagliatelle strips, allowing them to dry a little before supper began. Our only tool was the broom set between sink and worktop; the boys found this more than entertaining, particularly as we tried to keep each recipe separate so space was running out.

When supper began, with the chicken in cream sauce gently simmering, it was time to cook the pasta, each within its own pot. The look of anticipation on their faces was magical as we strained the waters away. Their sense of achievement was so strong, the dedication while creating, and now the pleasure of eating. Who was the winner? We decided it was a complete draw. A shake of the hands and a hug would do.

The true essence to this? I feel that my sons had learnt something very important in life. It was care and attention to detail, being patient for results, recognising one another's success and making sure it was acknowledged.

From one plus there's always a minus – they've both become Dad's biggest food critics!

Gary Rhodes is a chef, restaurateur, television presenter and cookery writer.

June Sarpong

The best advice my dad has ever given
me is, 'You become what you believe,
not what you want.'

This is the best advice anyone
has ever given me.

It's really important to keep a clear head and
think positively especially in tough times.

My dad is one of the most positive people
I know; I always turn to him for advice
both personally and professionally.

He's an all-round good guy.

June Sarpong is a television presenter.

Michael Simkins

My dad had the best job in the world for any kid: he owned a sweet shop at the seaside. He'd given up a career in the civil service before I was born after suffering a stomach ulcer through stress, and obviously decided that the life of a confectioner by the sea would be more restful. He was wrong, but it meant I had a blissful childhood.

Running a confectioner's (we also sold tobacco, newspapers and chemist's sundries) was so arduous and exhausting that he and Mum never really had time to check on how many sweets I was eating, and consequently I had full rein. As long as I didn't push my luck, I could have whatever I wanted, so by the age of six I could down a family-sized bottle of cream soda and a Crunchie bar in less than a minute. I may have been as large as a house, but I was never short of friends.

It was in the sweet shop too that Dad nurtured one of my great passions, that of cricket. Most nights, when the shop had emptied of customers, he'd stand behind the counter and bowl a tennis ball to where I stood in the well of the shop, clutching a child's bat and pretending to be Colin Milburn or Jim Parks. Eventually I became quite good, and thus his reward for all these hours of parental indulgence was the systematic demolition of his stock as I smote the ball to all parts: scuffing the greetings cards, knocking great dents in his chocolate gift boxes, and destroying his carefully prepared window displays. But he never complained.

Even better still, he was also in his spare time a very accomplished dance band musician. My earliest memories of him are of him going out on Friday and Saturday evenings with his tenor saxophone in the early 1960s to a gig at some swanky hotel or private party. Next day his tuxedo, hanging up by the stairs, would give off intriguing and exotic aromas of this other nocturnal life – cigars, hair gel, and the occasional heady scent of ladies' perfume. In his prime he resembled matinée idol Ronald Colman, and consequently was 'a bit of a dasher'.

Thus, 40 years on, the three great loves of my life are sweets, cricket and music. Which isn't a bad legacy for any parent to leave their son really. He was a fabulous, flawed, kindly man, with just a hint of roguishness. I miss him still.

Michael Simkins is an actor and author of What's My Motivation? *and* Fatty Batter.

Matthew Taylor MP

Working all hours. Weekends full of meetings. 'Free time' taken up talking shop and playing politics, or waiting for late-night votes in the Commons. Elected to Parliament almost straight out of university, this was the only life I knew. Captivating. Challenging. Addictive. And when we did get a few hours, it was a last-minute dash to the movies or hastily arranged meals out with friends. Summer trips back-packing in Africa, Asia, or Central America. Our time was 'us' time, Vicky and me.

Vicky and I were planning our first trip to India, looking forward to hopping on and off local buses and trains between Mumbai and Kerala, to soak up that very different culture. Then it happened. Sitting on the floor of the bathroom, we wept and laughed and hugged. Unplanned, unexpected, and the best news of our lives. The test was positive. We were having a baby.

In my 20 years in Parliament, I'd held most senior roles on offer in the Liberal Democrats, and suddenly the world refocused. A cliché – except it was real, and now, and us.

Being a dad has changed my life more for the better and to a greater degree than I could have ever imagined (and for Vicky, as mum, even more so). Did I say politics was captivating, challenging, and addictive? Arthur is more captivating. More challenging. More addictive.

For nine months we pored over *The Rough Guide to Having a Baby*, instead of *The Rough Guide to India*. Our first walk down the street with Arthur after he was born, just a week old, and London suddenly seemed every bit as noisy and busy and frantic as Calcutta.

I think pretty much every new father wants to be the best possible dad in the world. I guess we all have a slightly different idea of how to do it. All I knew was that I wanted 'Dad' to be as familiar, present and secure as 'Mum'. To be there, to help provide opportunities for him, to explore and discover the world as a family.

For me that has meant giving up politics come the next general election. With a Cornish constituency, I would have to be 280 miles away from the family four days a week. That, plus the late nights and working weekends, would have made me as much an absent dad as any 'ex'. That wouldn't be good enough. Not for Arthur!

Of course, I will still need to work. And Vicky wants to continue to have parts of her life that will be hers too. So we will share the care, and the work, and balance our lives as best we can. And already there is another baby on the way, and life will change again as we grow as a family. And even as I write, 11 months on, it seems extraordinary that life could change this much.

So this is being 'Dad'. Working all hours. Weekends full. Late nights. But now Arthur, and family, not politics and 'I', is the reason. Captivated. Challenged. Addicted. You bet. Oh, and exhausted. And very, very happy.

Matthew Taylor MP is Member of Parliament for Truro and St Austell, former Shadow Chancellor and former Party Chairman for the Liberal Democrats. His second son, Jacob, was born as this book went to press.

Lord Tebbit

My strongest memory of what it means
to be a father dates back to 1965, when
my wife became seriously ill following
the birth of our younger son.

I found myself not only father but mother
to him and his young brother and sister for
about three months. Fortunately my
employers (I was an airline pilot) decided
that I was so worried about my wife and
family that I was unfit to fly aeroplanes and
was put on indefinite sick leave.

From it all I learned that to be a complete
father you have to be ready to take on the
role of mother too. And I learned that I had
it much easier as a father than a mother.

Managing a seven-year-old and five-year-old and a new born baby is (and I know I am a wicked old sexist to say it) women's work.

But at least, as a red-blooded male (it was before I became a blue-blooded baron), I can hold my own in conversation in the queue at the checkout with any mother of three! Been there – done that, as they say.

Lord Tebbit is a former Cabinet Minister and former Member of Parliament for Chingford.

David Tennant

When you're a child you blithely assume that your dad knows everything. Now, aged 36, I have to admit that mine probably does. I don't mean he could rattle off the kings of England in order, or work out the quantity of dark matter in the universe on the back of a napkin (although he'd probably give it a good go): it's the dad stuff he's good at.

Problem with the car? Confusion over the house insurance? Need to put a shelf up? I'll call my dad.

Hardly a day will go by without that thought trundling through my head. And over the last ten years or so he's developed a bit of a flair for all things culinary, so you can now add, 'How do I blanch broccoli?' to the list.

He'll always have an answer, or at least know where to go to find one. (Anything involving gadgets, for instance, gets outsourced to his mate John who lives nearby in a house full of self-soldered circuit boards and half-built computers.) But it worries me. I'll be 40 in a few years – shouldn't I already know how to tile a bathroom wall? Where does Dad get all this knowledge from? Is it instinct? Was he born knowing how to replace a fan belt? Did he rely on *his* father for all these life skills? Were they passed down like an Olympic torch, practicality burning down the generations? Trouble is, I think I'm in danger of dropping it. When my kids phone *me* up to ask how to reignite their boiler I'll have to put them on to granddad.

I know it's not just me – my brother and sister are exactly the same.

Luckily, at 70 years of age, with one false hip, my dad, Sandy McDonald, is the most energetic, indefatigable man you are ever likely to meet.

Thank goodness for that. You've got years of cutting down trees and fixing curtain rails ahead of you, Dad. There's no peaceful retirement for you, I'm afraid. We'd be neck deep in chaos without you.

David Tennant is an actor and the current incarnation of Dr Who.

Margaret Thatcher

My father had always wanted to be a teacher, but coming from a family with limited means he had to leave school at 13 and earn his way – like so many other children in that first decade of the twentieth century. However, his passion for learning never dimmed nor did his belief that people could improve their lives through education.

This ethos was imprinted on me from a very early age. I was brought up in a household where reading was a central pastime. Each week my father would send me to the local library to collect a selection of books – classic novels, plays, poetry, biography, history or current affairs. And at the end of the week we would sit down to discuss them. He wanted each volume to add something to my knowledge. So we would talk about what I had enjoyed in the book. What lessons I had drawn from it. He taught me to develop my own conclusions and not to accept something just because others already had. So I learned to challenge the arguments, to test every conclusion –

and only then, when they passed examination, to accept them. It was a style of forensic questioning which I was to find extremely useful in my later political career.

The weekly diet of books, journals and newspapers which entered the Roberts' house also brought other advantages. I learned to read quickly and to absorb large amounts of written material. And the discipline of our weekly discussions meant that also I learned to memorise all the relevant information. Skills essential for a Prime Minister faced with a seemingly endless stack of Red Boxes!

Though Father enjoyed reading, he did not read simply for enjoyment. As a self-taught man he wanted to expand his knowledge of the world in order to play a fuller part in it. He read widely, but was discriminating in what he learned. Useful information would be stored away – at some stage to be used to bolster an argument in a Rotary discussion, to liven a speech at a town council meeting, or to enlighten a Sunday sermon in the Methodist Chapel. I too quickly picked up this habit of gathering up information, and throughout my political career I would regularly produce, from out of my handbag, a clipping from an obscure journal or a cutting from a little-read report, to catch out an unwary opponent or expose a badly prepared brief!

My father encouraged me and he pushed me. He wanted me to succeed academically where he had not. He made me understand that talent could be wasted if it wasn't matched by hard work. That ability, without the will to apply it, was a hollow quality. He was delighted when I went to Oxford – the culmination of so many of his hopes for me. Sadly, he did not live to see me become a Cabinet Minister, let alone Prime Minister. But I think he would have been proud of all I achieved and pleased that the example he had always tried to set had been such a sure and steadfast guide.

Margaret Thatcher was British Prime Minister from 1979 to 1990, and former leader of the Conservative Party.

Alan Titchmarsh

My dad was in many ways a classic
Yorkshireman. He sometimes didn't say
a lot – 'yes dear' was perhaps the phrase
most often used at home, but he wore the
trousers quietly all the same. He wore the
regulation bib-and-brace overalls for his
work as a plumber, topped by a tweed jacket
and a flat cap. I remember him smelling of
putty and blow-lamp fuel when he came
home from work, but for special occasions
he'd fill the bath to the brim, and boast
'no links' when he came down reeking of
'Old Spice' – having covered all the links
on the plug chain with water.

My dad died in 1986 at the early age of 62. It was a heart attack. So I had no chance to tell him what I thought of him, or to say goodbye. But I like to think he knew in what respect he was held. If he passed on anything to me, to use in my own role as a dad, it was a determination to be there for my children in difficult times. Not always to get it right, but at least to try. And every now and again, to tell them how much they mean to me.

I am a father of daughters, and I'm so relieved. I've never been good at football.

Alan Titchmarsh is a broadcaster, gardening expert, writer and novelist.

Arabella Weir

I guess I am, was, I have to say now, a daddy's girl. Whatever that means. My father certainly didn't buy me frilly dresses nor did he smile indulgently every time I opened my mouth – *au contraire*. I was, by no means, able to rely on my dad to champion my cause no matter what scrapes I got into. But we were always very close, increasingly so as I got older. However, the relationship was always at a distance – literally and metaphorically. My parents split up when I was eight and before that I really don't remember him being around much – being the early 1960s, he probably wasn't. Dads didn't do much childcare in those days. I assume he was busy steaming his way up the ladder at the Foreign Office. Really, thinking about it now, my real relationship with Dad started when my parents separated and for various reasons, out of his four children, only I went to live with him in the Middle East. Dad and I were kind of thrown together and our closeness started then. It's hard to describe Dad because in many ways he was so unlike a traditional father. He never gave advice, rarely listened to anything I was saying, didn't really follow my schoolwork and never went in for joint activities like bike riding or swimming. Erm, the only really dad-like thing I can recall him doing was shouting at me whilst I was doing a frantic front crawl in a swimming race, 'You've got to win!' Needless to say, I didn't.

Dad, like most Scotsmen, kept his praise and pride in his children to himself, occasionally letting a public acknowledgement of some of our achievements slip out – precious few as they were for me during my school days. He didn't go in for tender, loving words or for displays of affection. So, how did I know he loved me so much? How could I tell he adored me, if not via the more obvious signs? Well, by the gentle look in his eyes, the softening of his often somewhat impenetrable facial expression, the way he spontaneously and very uncharacteristically guffawed with laughter when I larked about. Thinking about it now, I got a taste for larking about endlessly as a child, and ultimately for a living, you might say, because it got such a great reaction from Dad, who could be pretty intellectually withering if you revealed ignorance on certain subjects.

When my father and I lived alone together in Bahrain, he'd make sure I was able, when appropriate, to tag along to all his engagements. As his adjunct, I met sheikhs, ate camel (cooked, by the way) off a kilim with my hands under a star-filled Arabian Gulf sky, and sat next to Edward Heath, amongst other unlikely but thrilling things for an under-ten-year-old. Dad was coming to terms with the divorce and I was his companion, although he never talked to me about adult matters, something for which I'll always be grateful. I might have been his little mate but I wasn't his confidante, thank God; he knew where to draw the line. His stoicism and sense of appropriateness meant he kept all the ghastliness that I later found out was going on between him and Mum to himself. So, that's something I learnt from him – hard as it often is when you're a parent, you have to be a grown-up around your kids. Now that I'm a mother, having, after many false tries, picked a decent man who is a wonderful dad, I realise that probably the most important thing I absorbed from my father, rather than learnt (because my dad certainly didn't set out to teach me this, I'm sure), was to value long-term commitment and loyalty. Dad might have been a long-distance dad most of my life, but he wrote regular, extremely loving letters – I always knew he was there, and just like my children's father, his kids came first and always would.

Arabella Weir is a comedian, actress and writer.

Fay Weldon

My dad was an archetypal kind of dad, a man of many adventures, glamorous. I adored him. He owned a copy of *Romeo and Juliet*, inscribed to him by Lawrence of Arabia: he'd been the latter's driver in World War One. I have a photo of him in army fatigues, leaning against one of those open-topped Rolls-Royces they used in desert warfare. He'd run away from home and joined up when he was 16. Everything connected with him seemed so rich and strange. He kept six small dusty stones in a row on his mantelpiece. When I was eight, I asked him why.

'They're not stones,' he said. 'They're gold nuggets. Gifts from grateful patients in lieu of money.'

And so they were. If you picked away with your fingernail, they gleamed. We spent the summers in Coromandel, in New Zealand's sub-tropical north: old goldminers still lurked in the kauri forests – stragglers from the gold rush, still bent on picking up nuggets from the forest floors – and apparently still succeeding. It was

Maori country: we went to school barefooted. My father was Medical Superintendent of the whole peninsula – my sister and I were known as 'the Doctor's daughters' and came in for a lot of respect. He was the peninsula's Superman. He'd take out appendixes on kitchen tables, deal with yaws, put on community plays – Ibsen's *Peer Gynt* was one, I remember – in the village hall of what was then little more than a ghost town, but is now a pleasure ground for tourists and hippies. Ever-anxious for our intellectual welfare, he would make us learn pages of John Stuart Mills by heart. Five sixpences a page for Mills, three for Shelley, one for Tennyson, as easier to learn. It was.

Rolled to starboard, rolled to larboard, when the surge was seething free.

Where the wallowing monster spouted his foam-fountains in the sea.

That was from 'The Lotus Eaters'. I earned four whole shillings. How can one forget that? I can quote it to this day. There was no end to his skills. When I hooked a blue shark, fishing from the Inspector of Fisheries' boat in the

Bay of Islands – he was looking for poachers on Gannet Island – it was my father who pulled it on board. Six foot long. He could do *anything*.

Fay Weldon is a novelist, short-story writer, playwright and essayist.

Robert Winston

My polymath father was a vibrant character – an expert violinist, a championship chess and bridge player, an actor and a spendthrift. His relationship with my mother was intense and loving, and their arguments were electrifying and full-blooded and, like everything else about my father, larger than life. When he took up archery, during bad weather he practised by firing numerous heavy arrows across the dining room. One night he had a massive row with my mother about some trivia. After chasing her around the dining-room table, he picked up his cup of cocoa and threw it at my mother's head. My athletic mother ducked in time and the cup hit the pock-marked dining-room wall, shattered, and left thick streaks of brown cocoa.

Breakfast next morning was a sombre, heads-down affair. Nobody spoke for a long time as the cornflakes and toast were passed round. Finally, my father looked up and said, 'You know – I've been thinking – it's about time we had this room redecorated.' He died a year later when I was just nine, and my mother was devastated.

Professor Lord Winston is a doctor, scientist and broad-caster, renowned for his pioneering work in the field of reproductive medicine.

Alan Yentob

At first sight my dad was awesome to behold. A mane of silver-grey hair, swept back like two small hills on either side of his forehead. Eyebrows so bushy a small animal could find refuge there. A comical bulbous nose, reminiscent of W. C. Fields...And a face so craggy and characterful he could have lived in it for a thousand years.

If you were a small child his appearance could be pretty intimidating...And his name, Isaac Reuben Yentob, was a perfect match. Sat in a corner of the living room in his comfortable armchair, he looked like an Old Testament prophet presiding over a motley crew of children, relatives and hangers-on. Our house was like Babel, with an endless stream of visitors drifting in and out. Many of them had arrived from far away without the means to make a living, speak the language or fend for themselves. So inevitably they would stay a week, a month...or more.

The women of the house, my mother and her sisters, were always busy preparing delicious food, and the cooking smells, exotic and oriental, drifted through the rooms mingling with the laughter and cries of children and the babble of house guests talking animatedly in English, French and Arabic. Meanwhile my father, the silent benefactor, took it all in his stride, remote, unruffled in the haven of his armchair...Until that is...nightfall when an astonishing transformation took place and our dad, the diffident patriarch of 5 Moorfield Road, turned into a flamboyant musical impresario as captivating in his own way as the Pied Piper of Hamelin.

Born and bred in Iraq, he left along with many other Jews after World War Two, but he brought with him to Manchester where we lived a love of Arabic music and the haunting sounds of the oud (the Arab equivalent of the lute) and the tabla (a small, cone-shaped drum).

On the flimsiest excuse he would arrange a chalry, a spontaneous musical evening not unlike a ceilidh to which everyone and anyone was invited. My dad played the tabla cross-legged on the floor, his fingers tapping rhythmically, joyously on the tiny drum, his body rocking back and forth, his face radiating all the warmth and expressiveness notably absent in daylight hours. He was transfigured and we children were transfixed as he and my brilliant Uncle Naim on the oud got into their stride and entertained us with song after song after song...

And that's how I shall remember my dad until the day I die.

Alan Yentob is BBC Creative Director, and a television programme maker and presenter.

Toby Young

It started out as possibly the worst day of my life.

I had applied to Brasenose College, Oxford, to read Philosophy, Politics and Economics, and the previous week I'd received a letter from the College Secretary telling me what time to arrive, where to pick up my room key, and so on. It wasn't addressed to me personally – it began 'Dear Candidate' – but because it was clearly a form letter sent out to successful applicants, I assumed I'd got it. I was astonished – not least because I hadn't met the conditional offer that the College had given me. I went round telling everyone. The teachers at the North London comprehensive I'd attended couldn't believe it. I was one of only two people to get into Oxford that year.

Then, that morning, I received a letter from the College Admissions Tutor – this one addressed to me personally. He expressed his condolences that I'd failed to meet his 'extremely generous' conditional offer, conveyed his regrets about not being able to offer me a place at Brasenose and wished me luck in my university career 'elsewhere'.

The first thing I did was show it to my father who was sitting opposite me at the breakfast table.

'But I thought you said you'd got in?'

'Yes, well, I got a letter implying I had.'

He asked to see the first letter and, after running his eye over it, suggested he call the Admissions Tutor to find out which of the letters was correct.

'But, Dad, the second one's the correct one. The first one's obviously a mistake.'

'Maybe, maybe not. Let's call him and see.'

I was absolutely adamant that he shouldn't call – 'There's no point, it'll just be embarrassing' – but he was equally insistent that he should. I pleaded with him not to, but there was no stopping him. He had the bit between his teeth.

He used the phone in his study and I stood beside him trying to listen.

He explained what had happened to the Admissions Tutor and asked him to clarify the situation.

'We can't offer Toby a place because he didn't meet

the conditional offer,' he explained. Then, after a pause, he asked, 'Which letter did he get first?'

'The one implying he'd got in,' said my father.

'Hang on a minute, I'm actually in a meeting with the PPE tutors right now. Let me discuss it with them.'

At this point my father took the phone away from his ear and held it between us so we could both hear what was being said. Incredibly, the tutors launched into a discussion about whether sending me the letter implying I'd got in created a moral obligation on their part to offer me a place. It was oddly reminiscent of the sort of questions I'd been asked during my one-hour interview six months earlier.

After the tutors had gone back and forth about this for approximately five minutes, the Admissions Tutor came back on the line.

'Okay,' he said. 'He can come.'

After I'd got over my jubilation, I realised that my father had taught me a valuable lesson: no matter how unlikely you are to succeed, you should never – ever – give up. My father was a social entrepreneur and it was a principle he adhered to all his life. It enabled him to set up dozens of organisations, such as the Social

Science Research Council, many of them against appalling odds. He never accepted no for an answer – not if there was the slightest chance of persuading someone to change their mind.

And with one phone call he changed my life.

Toby Young is a journalist, playwright and the author of How to Lose Friends and Alienate People.

THE GENETIC FACTOR

Dr Jane Zuckerman

Was it the environment or genetic factors? For as long as I can remember, I always wanted to follow in my father's footsteps. This was fostered in many various ways, numerous visits to his laboratories and going to staff children's parties at the London School of Hygiene and Tropical Medicine, which sowed the early seeds of wishing to practise medicine, but perhaps mostly by the unique opportunities I had as a child to travel together with my father, just the two of us.

I have overriding memories of two particularly unforgettable trips, both of which influenced me in different ways. The first trip was to America, a whistle-stop tour from east to west with a few days' stopover in Chicago, on my mother's suggestion that I accompanied my father on this 'business trip' instead of her. This was not a business trip as most people would know it, rather a journey enjoying the sights of New York, Washington and San Francisco, mixed with giving keynote lectures at an important medical conference in Chicago. I firmly believe that I imbibed the heady mixture of clinical and academic medicine while sitting quite well-behaved at the back of conference rooms, looking, listening and, without really realising, learning the skill required to teach and train medicine. I very often see that I am quite simply the mirror image of my father, at least professionally speaking!

I was all of 11 years old when we travelled together to America; I have a vivid recollection of going to the top of the Empire State Building, visiting the Guggenheim Museum and the Smithsonian Institute Museums, shopping at Marshall Field's in Chicago, all of which inevitably contributed to me becoming a rounded person and being taught by my father to appreciate other things in life than just medicine. The *pièce de résistance* of this trip, though, was an unexpected journey to San Francisco courtesy of ITV who wished to film my father for a television documentary. Not only was I enthralled to see all this live and in action, but somehow my father managed to engineer a tour of San Francisco in a chauffer-driven limousine which made me feel quite the star of the trip.

As I grew older, the other journey I recall was to Geneva where my father went frequently to the World Health Organisation (WHO). I not only wandered around the wonderful city, but also around WHO, and it fills me with enormous pride that I have literally followed in my father's footsteps as I myself now collaborate with WHO.

The underlying confidence to succeed that both my father and my mother have instilled in me continues, and is a reflection of all the encompassing experiences I had during my very memorable childhood. However, counter these impressions with the elements of a determination to succeed and to make a difference, and I must conclude that both my upbringing and genetic factors have made me the person I am. The fact that inevitably emerges is that 'genes will ultimately show'.

Dr Jane Zuckerman is a consultant in travel medicine and vaccines, Royal Free and University College Medical School.

ONE OF THE GREAT MEN OF BOTSWANA
Alexander McCall Smith

Precious Ramotswe thought of her father, the late Obed
Ramotswe, every day – without fail. It was not that she
regarded this as a duty, as some people do when they
remember their parents. No, she thought of him because
she felt so proud of him, and because he was there with
her in the land that she saw about her. He was her father,
but he was also her country.

'Tell me about your late daddy,' said Mma Makutsi
once, as they were driving down to Lobatse in Mma
Ramotswe's tiny white van. 'I know that you think of
him; you have told me that. But tell me about him.'

Mma Ramotswe shifted at the wheel of the tiny white
van, which listed to starboard, her side. 'He had a hat,'
she said.

Mma Makutsi glanced at her. Many people had hats,

even if rather fewer these days than in the past. 'And, Mma?'

'He had a very old hat,' said Mma Ramotswe. 'He had a very old hat with a brim that was almost detached from the crown. It was held together with two safety pins. He could easily have afforded a new hat, but he did not want to part with the hat he had.'

This made them both smile.

'And he loved cattle,' she went on. 'He was one of those people who could remember every cow he had ever had – he never forgot even one of them. They were like family to him. He knew the mother and father of each member of the herd, and who the grandparents were. He taught me to tell a good cow from a bad cow and to get rid of the bad ones. But he never tried to sell a bad cow to somebody without telling them that she was bad. He would say, "This is not a good one, and I will charge you less for her." That is what he would say.'

Mma Makutsi thought about this. 'Why can't car dealers be like that, Mma Ramotswe?'

Mma Ramotswe smiled. 'They are a different breed of people, I think, Mma. And I think that they have forgotten the old Botswana ways.'

For a little while they were silent, each lost in their individual thoughts. Then Mma Ramotswe said, 'I dream of him, you know, Mma. I dream that my late daddy is no longer late. I dream that he is with me. We go out walking, you know, in this dream of mine. We are in the bush, and my daddy is walking in front of me, wearing his hat. And I feel so proud that he can see now what we have done with our country – what we have made of it. But I also want to find out what it is like, in that place where he is now. That place.'

She took a hand off the wheel and waved it vaguely, in a direction between the dry hills in the distance and the sky.

Mma Makutsi thought: this is the question that we should all like answered. This is the question. 'And what does he say, Mma?' she asked.

'He says there are cattle there,' said Mma Ramotswe. 'Fine white cattle, with sweet breath and cattle bells about their necks. And there is good rain for the grass. And it is just like Botswana, he says.'

'And does he wear a new hat in that place, I wonder,' said Mma Makutsi.

'No,' said Mma Ramotswe. 'Same Daddy.' And then she added, 'Same hat.'

She realised that she was crying. And why not? Why should I not cry, she asked? Why should anybody not cry for their daddy?

'He was such a good man,' she said, between her sobs.

The tiny white van slowed down, swerved once or twice, and then continued its journey as before.

Alexander McCall Smith is renowned for his much-loved No. I Ladies' Detective Agency *series of novels.*

Sarah Brown is President of the charity PiggyBankKids which she founded in 2002. PiggyBankKids supports a wide range of charitable projects which create opportunities for children and young people, and has launched the Jennifer Brown Research Fund to seek solutions to pregnancy and premature birth difficulties and help save newborn lives. She is also patron of a number of charities addressing healthcare and women's issues including Wellbeing of Women, Women's Aid, Maggie's Cancer Caring Centres and the White Ribbon Alliance for Safe Motherhood. Sarah is married to the British Prime Minister Gordon Brown. They live in London and Fife with their sons John and Fraser.

Gil McNeil is the bestselling author of *The Only Boy For Me*, *Stand By Your Man*, *In the Wee Small Hours* and *Divas Don't Knit*. She helps run the charity PiggyBankKids, and lives in Canterbury with her son.

PiggyBankKids is a charity which creates opportunities for children and young people who would otherwise miss out. An umbrella charity, running a number of projects, we often work in partnership with other charities. All our work is in the UK.

PiggyBankKids' work includes:

The Jennifer Brown Research Fund

At the Jennifer Brown Research Laboratory, led by Professor Andrew Calder, a talented and dedicated team of scientists are advancing pioneering research projects that are making real life progress towards resolving some of the life-threatening complications that can arise during pregnancy. The fund finances five separate research projects – looking at placental function, pre-eclampsia, the impact of infection on premature labour, the causes of blindness in premature babies and exploring oxygen fluctuations in reducing incidences of brain damage in premature babies.

The Jennifer Brown Research Fund also supports small innovative schemes such as the Granny school, a project piloted in Fife which is a refresher course for first-time grand-parents, and which has been so successful it will be rolled out to other areas across the UK. Other innovative projects include the play-away bus and a community research project on postnatal depression.

Mentoring

PiggyBankKids supports a wide range of amazing children's charities providing opportunities for vulnerable young people around the UK. Chance UK seeks to provide an early and transforming intervention in vulnerable children's lives so that, together with their families, they can build a brighter future. It provides targeted solution-focused mentoring for children aged five to eleven, based on individual needs. To support the work of mentoring charities we published *Moving On Up* in 2002, where famous people wrote about the mentors who had most influenced their lives. Free copies of *Moving On Up* were sent to every state and independent secondary school in the UK.

Competing

Special Olympics is an international non-profit organisation dedicated to empowering individuals with intellectual disabilities to become physically fit, productive and respected members of society through sports training and competition. In 2005 we published *Journey to the Sea*, a collection of new fiction and travel writing, to support the work of Special Olympics Great Britain.

The Big Night In

To support our projects the Big Night In was devised for those who want to do something for charity, but don't have time to train for a marathon or walk the Great Wall of China. Money raised during the Big Night In goes directly to projects ranging from the Jennifer Brown Research Fund to mentoring and family support services and charities focusing on improving sports provision for vulnerable young people.

For further information please contact:

Joe Hewitt

Project Manager

PiggyBankKids

PO Box 61041

London SE1 9RF

020 7556 6855

You can read more about PiggyBankKids projects at:

www.piggybankkids.org